# Life,

## AIN'T IT GREAT,
### and how to enjoy it.

TONY BOVI

authorHOUSE®

*AuthorHouse™ LLC*
*1663 Liberty Drive*
*Bloomington, IN 47403*
*www.authorhouse.com*
*Phone: 1-800-839-8640*

*Published by AuthorHouse    04/16/2014*

*ISBN: 978-1-4969-0229-0 (sc)*
*ISBN: 978-1-4969-0228-3 (e)*

*Library of Congress Control Number: 2014906455*

<u>**This book is dedicated to:**</u>

*In memory of Mom & Dad,*

*For my loving wife,*

*All my children,*

*Entire family, present, and past,*

*All my friends, and*

*Everyone, who knowingly and unknowingly,*
*crossed my path at some point in time,*

*You all had a part in supplying the material for this and other*
*writings. Without all of you, this would not be possible.*

# INTRODUCTION

It all began the day after Christmas a couple of years ago. Seeing the demolition of a living room, the stacks of crumpled paper on the floor, and the need to face the throngs at the stores for returns or exchanges, a thought occurred on how this affects everyone regardless of religion or beliefs. We are going to live through this day. It sparked so many thoughts that it became necessary to record them in a journal.

It was a hobby of mine to go to the mall on that day, buy a cup of coffee, and a hot cinnamon roll. I would find a seat in center court, and watch the craziness that happens. I would watch the people frantic with their goals, finding the sales, searching for the bargain of the year, or finding the right size. They would be yelling at the kids in tow or crazily searching for those who slipped out of range. Her glares at her husband who bought the wrong size, but in return, his glares at his wife who bought the tie and not golf balls. Out in the mall the dismantling of the Christmas decorations and assembly of Valentine's Day pieces had started. The activity is enough to fill reams of paper. This is why I find it so interesting. It is life, and, to me, there is nothing more fascinating.

This journal became the dumping ground for a multitude of stories when the series began with posting them on Facebook, which lead to Twitter, Google, and Tumbr. They started out as one or two sentences, but some grew to be short stories. There would be days when the pages were empty, but then there were days that never ended. Everything enclosed comes from the heart, but the other sources might include a thought, a quote, or a memory. Some of the stories are either food for development into children's books or a steamy novel. They are what go through the head at that moment.

This is the reason why there is not a flow of thought from one day to the next. Each daily entry is different because this mind does not produce a continuous story day after day. It could be equivalent to a diary of sorts. Whatever is on the brain when the feet hit the floor in the morning is what ends up on paper. One day it might be a family memory and the next a lecture on overcoming a bad mood and yet the following day being a shopping trip. If you are looking for a plot or storyline, this book is not for you. If you are searching for entertainment, education, or inspiration, and, at times, faith, then this is just right. Someone once said, my writings would be great for people with Attention Deficit Disorder (ADD) because if the read becomes boring just flip to the next page.

As a professional disclaimer, I am not a Social Worker, Therapist, Psychologist, or Analyst. I majored in Business Administration. The only professional help I can offer is inspirational, motivational, and storytelling based on personal experiences. If you are seeking professional services, this is not the place to receive it. I am here to tell it as it is in my life and the lives of all who have touched my heart, of whom amount to thousands. Some I personally know, but most I do not.

My childhood was as normal as any, but there are certain aspects of it that stayed in my mind and, for some reason, are a part of this compilation. My one company career of thirty-three years took me to places I thought I would never experience. I met wonderful people around the world many of who are still friends, some are no longer with us, and some will always be in my memory for one reason or another. After all is said, this was my education in life. If you were looking for someone who could hold a doctorate in life, I would be a candidate.

My philosophy about life is simple and easy. We have to be the most important person to ourselves. If we are not, then our value to anyone else is nothing. Another thought is to live life to the fullest. We are here on this earth to blow the top off our existence, so in the end we are all we have left.

A suggestion for those who like an entry and want to bookmark it, I suggest buying a packet of index tabs or sticky notes at the local market or office supply house, and tag the page. This way you can refer back to it. Another use for them is to mark those pages to omit without tearing them out. This option is totally your choice.

If all of this makes sense, then continue with caution and an open mind.

## The Day after Christmas

The day after . . . , bags of paper and boxes, recycle bin over flowing, garbage lids not fitting properly, kitchen needs a major overhaul, floors barely navigational, and think, 5 days to prepare for a New Year's Party. HELP!!!!! Is this the thought that runs through our minds this day of the year? Well, the reassuring fact is, we are not alone.

If we spent the same amount of energy on doing the things we want as we did coming up with reasons why we should not, we would never have regrets. It is just a little food for thought to start the day.

## No Straight Path

Throughout our lifetime, we face roadblocks, obstacles, bumps, curves, and so on. There are also forks, exits, ramps, and dividers to navigate. The maps, directions, and GPS need following. Throughout this entire journey and no matter which device we choose always remember this is the path that led us to what we are today. Make that journey a memorable one.

## Today and Everyday

At this point everything in this year's calendar are noted such as national holidays, religious holidays, birthdays, anniversaries, weddings, special days to remember, and maybe even trash day. They are all there for a reason, to remember.

The empty space left on that calendar allows us to fill it with whatever we wish. We should live our life as if it was a blank canvas, and we are the artist. Paint that masterpiece!

## Envy Maybe?

Why do we try so hard to fit into other peoples' lives when our own life has so much to offer? Their life may not be the greatest on the inside, but, at least, we know what we have. If we do not know, find out. It could be the greatest adventure for us ever.

**Housekeeping**

Today we are going to do some housekeeping:
1. Place a huge box in the middle of the room
2. Gather up all the worries, heartaches, sorrows, pains, anger, hatred, disappointments, sadness, bad friendships, anything you can find that effected your year, or years in some cases
3. Pack them in this box, if extra boxes are needed, that's okay.
4. Get some packing tape and close them up tight.
5. At midnight, you are going through the door marked tomorrow, and leave all that baggage behind.

**Feelings**

Did you know you control your own feelings? It took many years and many therapy sessions to make this conclusion. At that exact time when this paradigm shift happened, I decided to be happy all the time. That really pisses some people off, but then again, I cannot control their feelings either . . . Oh well, it sucks to be them.

**Past**

If we continue to live in the past, that is a waste of our life. We need to forgive, forget, let go, adjust, or just plainly start over because today is here to be lived, and tomorrow is worth anticipating. It is good to have memories, but do not try to relive them.

**Live Today**

It took a lifetime for us to arrive at today. We must have done something right; otherwise, we would not be sitting where we are right now. Give thanks to all those people who helped us along the way. Their presence in our life made the difference. Man, that ride is great; we cannot let it pass without enjoying and sharing it.

## Children

An old grump of a relative once said, "Children should be seen, not heard." If you cannot hear the sound of laughter and happiness and the words "I love you," you have missed the reason for living.

## Helping

Every journey begins with the first step. For some, that step is easy, but for others, it is one of the most difficult things to do. If we assure them that we will help, it may make it easier. Help someone today. Not only will they love you for it, but it will help you too.

## Love

I always thought that loving yourself was being selfish and egotistical, but I found that you need to do this in order to love anyone else. There is a difference between self-adoration and self-love. Love is one of the greatest gifts we have. It is too bad we sometimes don't treat it that way.

## Time

As opposed to the theory that time is money. Time is actually a precious gem and mainly used to expand our life, our love, and our happiness. Take time to live life to its fullest potential every minute of the everyday. We should never be aware of time until we are running late. It is usually an indicator that we are just having too much fun living it.

## Judgment Day

When our final day comes, and we are at the pearly gates, we are judged on not what we had, but what we did with what we had. That is the priority, so money and riches are nothing after life, only blessings. The more of those we have, the happier we will be not only here but also after.

## Positive Living

Wow! Every morning is incredible. A new day, a fresh start, healthy, happy, loved, and love, there is nothing that can stop us now. Positivity generates energy and every day we can charge up with it. Negativity is one of the most energy consuming forces, so if we feel drained, it may be time to think positive again and enjoy the day.

## Impatience

Impatience may be our worse enemy. We all want everything done and done now. Unemployment, new house, promotion, raises, new car, new furniture, vacations, bills paid up, dinner, this book, etc. all need to be done now sometimes at any expense.

Close your eyes, take a deep breath, count to ten, slowly let the breath out, and relax. Everything in our lives takes time such as birth, healing, love, growth, faith, strength, living, and, yes, cooking. So give time, time to develop. All good things are worth waiting for.

## Touch Someone

Stop and think about how many people we actually touch in some way, every day. The people we meet on the bus going to work, walking with people into work, people at work, the grocery store, laundry, walking and so on, are all people with whom we come in contact. If we leave one with a smile and a happy heart, we have accomplished our purpose.

## Kids

Freshly fallen snow should bring out the kid in us. It is never too late to throw a snowball or build a snowman. Remember, we are all kids until . . .

## Falling Snow

The peaceful quiet of freshly falling snow is quite therapeutic in so many ways. The overall quiet in the air, deaden sounds of a car, the light floating flakes as they land on the ground are all sounds of peace. Let's close our eyes and let our minds carry us to all our peaceful thoughts.

## Imagination

Imagination is one thing we cannot teach our children because they already have it. We just need to help them develop it into what they see themselves being and never discourage them from being just that. Let them be who they believe they can be.

## Fitting In

Why do people try so hard to be something they are not? If it means trying to be accepted, maybe those are not the people or places for you. Any energy exertion of trying should raise a red flag.

## Impacting Life

I was brought up to make an impact on others, at the same time; I learned how others make an impact on me. Those that were good, I kept. The others, I discarded. Just sayin'.

## Conforming

If we are always trying to conform, we are giving up the most important factor in life, US. Being our self is far easier than working so hard to be someone they want us to be. This may not be who we really are.

## Nice Day

When I say to someone "It's a nice day," and they reply, "What's so good about it," I respond with "All my blessings, good health, good weather, loving children, and grandchildren, and . . ." I do not even come close to finishing when that person walks away. Why would they do that? They are the one who asked, and I am just answering their question.

## Dumb Things

When I laugh at the dumb things I do, it makes me think. I am not too proud to share my stupidity with others. I figure if they laugh with me, then I have accomplished two things. One, I've made them happy, and two, they are not laughing at anyone else.

## Love

Love is the greatest gift ever because it is free, and the more we give the more we receive. It is more precious than the most valuable gem or all the money in the world. Never be afraid to share love; expect to fall into love; but most important is that we need to let everyone know how much we love them.

## Reflections

Have you ever made time to step back and take a GOOD look at yourself? Are you proud of what you see? Do not look at your accomplishments (past) or how much you have (material) or what you have become (ego). Those are not important. Look at who you REALLY are, and what you believe. I hope you see something wonderful.

## The Seed of Love

Love is like a seed, once planted it grows with time. If treated properly:

. . . it is exciting, so you will always live each day fully.
. . . it is fun, so you always laugh out loud and play like a child.
. . . it is with you always, so you are never alone.
. . . it never matures, so it keeps you young and vibrant.
. . . it never dies, so you take it with you from here to beyond.

If you have love, take care of it, and it will take care of you.

## Giving

Today is a good day to give to others. It is not an expense, just us. Make someone smile; it always improves a person's outlook. Make someone laugh, it might give them the spirit they need. Give them a listening ear; they may need to talk something through. Give a hug, a kiss, or just the words "I care," it may make a difference for them at that moment. If we do this, our day will be ten times better and, most importantly, so will theirs. Try it.

## Friends

Good friends are irreplaceable. They are the ones who will stand by you throughout any type of adversity. They are also the ones who you want to be with no matter what the circumstance. They are also the ones who will not talk behind your back and will always tell you what you need to hear, and you feel the same back. They are the ones who will tell you, "Your ass looks big in that," and you will listen and not get mad. God bless all my friends.

## Talking About . . .

There is not a day that passes when I read or hear about one person bashing another. It makes me cringe to think that it may be caused by the way they look or dress or what they said or the accent they have or how they act or what they believe in or don't believe in or simply how they walk. I am not saying that it is wrong to have your own feelings or opinions, but expressing them and how they are expressed is the sign of maturity and compassion.

## Rough Times

The one great thing about rough times is that we know it is going to get better, but it only depends on us making it that way. If we are always waiting for someone else, our recovery is a long ways away. We are the only ones who can make a difference. Faith, trust, and perseverance are what it takes.

## Fresh Start

Every day we wake up to a blank page to build our creation. Throughout the day, we make mistakes, have problems, list our great ideas, tell wonderful love stories, share with friends, see the beauty of the day, . . . ,and at the end of the day, do we have a full or empty page. It is all in our hands to create our day as we see fit.

## Love

Like money, love grows if invested properly, but the ultimate difference is that love, if given, received, and cared for, compounds so fast that it becomes overwhelming. The absolute greatest gift to give anyone is love from the heart, and it does not cost a penny.

It is a beautiful day to love others. Practice it. Try it. Accept it, so it becomes something that is permanent.

## Letting Go

When you can ignore your ego, refuse to being right all the time, stop comparing yourself to others, and just be satisfied with what you have and who you are, only then can you begin to find peace within. Try it. You may like it.

## Popular Vote

I am not a political person, nor will you hear me promote one candidate over another. I heard something that upset me tremendously today. The statement, "I am voting for this candidate because everyone else is." If this were the case, we would not be Americans today; we would still be a British colony. Do you think that the majority of the people back then wanted to fight, be injured, or killed? I think not.

Friends, we vote for whom WE think is going to be the best person for the job regardless of what anyone else thinks. The reason we vote is to voice OUR opinion, NOT to voice the majority.

People do not realize they are doing more harm than good. If the person who is the "poll leader" was in favor of eliminating the deficit by doing away with everyone over the age of 85 because it cost too much to support them, and the majority used the "favorite candidate" thought process, our parents and grandparents would no longer exist. Agreed, this is an extreme example; however, it is just like following those who do not want you to think for yourself and let the majority do it for you. God gave us a brain; the government gave us the right to vote our conscience. USE IT!!!

**Love and Passion**

Love and passion are stronger than any drug on the market. Pharmaceutical companies have been trying for years to improve it in one way or another. How do you improve perfection?

**Wonderful Day**

When I woke up this morning, the wind was blowing, my recycle bin was swirling around the backyard, the coffee maker leaked water all over the kitchen counter and floor, what coffee was made tasted like espresso, my cell phone was warning me of the wind advisory . . . HOWEVER, the sun is shining and love is in my heart.

The wind is only temporary, the recycle bin can be tied down, the coffee maker can be replaced, the counter and floor can be mopped up, Dunkin' Donuts® is down the street, tomorrow the coffee will be better, and the phone can be silenced. I have been granted this beautiful day to live life to its fullest. WHO IS BETTER THAN ME?

**Bright Days:**

It does not take a speech to change someone's day. Just a few words in any language can do just that.

"I'm sorry."
"I forgive you."
"You look beautiful."
"Can I help?"

"Here's a hug."
"I love you."

How often do you use them? Change someone's day about whom you care. It will also help you.

## Negativity vs. Positivity

NEGATIVITY is infectious. It spreads to others and can cause the demise of relationships, friendships, and businesses. It can also promote loneliness, isolationism, and a distorted view of everything. It can also lead to poor health and depression. Some people miss brand it as reality.

On the other hand, POSITIVITY is also an infection; however, it benefits love, relationships, and strong ties to others. It also promotes togetherness, attraction, and emits an aura of goodness. Some people call it daydreaming, BUT I call it reality with a bright future.

## Love Our Self

It is written that we must love our self before we can love anyone else. I always thought of this as a self-centered and egotistical thing. Then it occurred to me, if I do not respect myself, care for myself, believe in myself, stand up for myself, and like who I am, then how can I show the same to everybody else?

I thank God everyday for my parents who brought me up showing me how to love as they did. Let us teach our children how it is done, and, maybe, things will turn around in this world.

## Emotions

Our emotions are like garbage in a wastebasket. They keep piling up and up until it overflows. Sometimes, we leave it there so long it begins to smell and creates a cloud over us. It is only when we realize that all we needed to do was empty it out, occasionally, to clear the air. Do not hold on to your emotions, empty it, and start fresh every night. You will sleep better and live longer and happier.

**Truly Good Friend**

Sometimes the only things needed are a good set of ears for listening, a soft shoulder to lean on, and gentle arms for a hug. It is truly a good friend who knows when to and when not to be there.

**Last Words**

If you have only one thing to say to a loved one before you pass away, what would you say and whom would you direct it to?

Mine would be "I LOVE YOU AND WILL CARRY THAT LOVE WITH ME TO THE NEXT LIFE UNTIL WE CAN SHARE IT AGAIN." Friends, and never miss a chance to say, "I love you."

**Cold Air**

When I think about getting out of bed, I ponder the thought of leaving this warm and cozy environment to face the reality of the February air in New England, getting out of the shower, putting on cold clothes, the chilling morning air inside, walking outside to feel that cold hitting my face, getting into a cold car, greeting people with cold hands, etc., these are all things that make me shiver.

As the alternative, the greatest part about all of it is, I AM ALIVE AND BREATHING, and well enough to realize how I should approach the day. I plan to have a fantastic day, and I hope you do too.

**Beauty**

If I truly open my eyes to things all around, I can find beauty. It is what I let my eyes see, my mind create, and my heart feel. This is the most serene moment I have every day. Try to take time to SEE the beauty all around and be thankful that we can.

## Obstacles

In life, everyone has to plow through his or her own form of crap. The important thing is:

How we look at it?
How we deal with it?
How we plan to overcome it?

Do we put our head down and plow through it; or do we let it happen to us? If it is you who have these things to contemplate, try putting your head down and charge forward. There is nothing to lose.

## Decisions

There are times in our lives when we reach a crossroads and decisions must be made. These decisions might mean EVERYTHING to us and our family; counseling vs. divorce, short sale vs. foreclosure, a battle with creditors vs. bankruptcy, adoption vs. abortion, or life vs. suicide.

Someone is contemplating these decisions every day. Do we know them? It could be as close as the person sitting next to us. Pray that they make a decision what will be beneficial for not only them but also everyone else around them. Let us keep our eyes and ears open because we could possibly make a difference.

## Silence

Sometimes saying nothing is the best policy. If words are spoken inappropriately, it can cause hurt feelings, pain, anger, animosity, shock, devastation, burnt bridges, and depression. It can also have repercussions that may affect love, friendships, credibility, honor, reliability, confidence, and mainly perception from all others.

It is not the point of pleasing or compromising anything, but a point of knowing down deep what is right. It takes maturity to control the mouth and know what and when it should be said, if at all. Some never reach that point in their lives. It disturbs me to know there are children that know better than adults do.

## Equals

I have never understood how people feel that they are better than anyone else is. Outside of the obvious differences of financial, social status, career position, value of "toys," refinement, amount of riches, illnesses, disparity, etc., I could probably make a list longer than a roll of toilet paper single-spaced.

The point being, we are all human beings. We all require the same care, nutrition, protection, hygiene, and attention. Yet there is such a stratification of levels within our society, socially and politically, even though "WE ARE ALL CREATED EQUAL." Think about it.

## Trivia

Why do people make trivial things into the most monumental disasters of the century? I mean these are pointless items. The basis is not a nuclear explosion, downfall of humanity, or failed resolve to the economic crisis. I am talking about not getting the order for their coffee correct, getting the perfect parking spot at the market, assigned the perfect seat at the theatre, or as simple as why the toilet seat was left up (been there, done that, in a previous life).

Well, other things need more attention than this crap. If we spent half the time on what needs our attention, there would be peace in this world and global prosperity.

## Smile

If we could reach out to one person every day to turn a frown into a smile, do you realize how many smiles we would have created in a lifetime. This gift cannot be matched by anything.

Here is a daily checklist to start the day to put smiles on faces:

Happy song in mind to hum
Dancing shoes on
Party clothes on
Smile on face

Now go out, greet the world, and make at least one-person smile, if not hundreds.

## Finding Love

I have a theory about love. When you are looking for love, you will never find the right one. It is when you least expect it, love will find you.

You love your friends. Did you specifically go looking for them, probably not? When the time is right, not only for you, but also for that special person to walk into your life or, for that matter, you walk into theirs, IT will find you. Let it grow and enjoy its beauty.

Saturday is time to enjoy life. For some it is the last day of work. For others, it is a day to clean the garage, basement, attic, etc. For some, it is your day of rest. The one thing that it is for everyone, it is a day to love one another with all your heart (as everyday should be). If Hallmark® can create special days, why can't we?

## Listen

Do you have friends who just cannot seem to talk about anything but themselves? Some have nothing to talk about at all, but others are looking for confirmation that they are leading the life they should. In any of these cases, they need someone to listen to them. Be patient, loving, and understanding no matter how much you want to walk away. THAT is a good friend.

On the seventh day, He rested. He didn't say anything about daylight savings time, but He still rested.

**Lulu's Eulogy:**

My oldest son, his wife and two sons had a huge change in their lives today. Their best friend and only four-legged daughter, Lulu, was put to sleep this morning after she struggled in and out of sickness for some time. Lulu was not only an English Bull Dog, but also a very special one at that. Lulu was the beginning of their family before the two-legged ones were even thought of and continued to consider herself as the only daughter they never had.

When their two sons were born, Lulu was instrumental in being the watchdog throughout their infant stages. She would lay at the doorway of their rooms listening to every move they made. As heavy as she was and slobbering she might have been, she was always taken care of with the love and attention of their natural children.

She would attend all family functions including the great-grandparent's 60th wedding anniversary. Outside of their party, Lulu was the "Belle of the Ball." She did not go without a pet or scratch. She was always the first one to greet you at the front door and the last one to bid you farewell.

She will be laid to rest in a peaceful spot on family land, thanks to my daughter-in-law's parents who loved and cared for Lulu as their own. She will be missed tremendously by all. She was a major part of our lives in many ways, not only for her unique demeanor, but also for her loving nature. She will be taken care of in the next life, by her great-grandparents. She will be safe.

God bless you little girl. You lived a live worth barking about. We will all miss you, but you will be happier than ever before.

**Final Journey**

Every minute of every day is a journey. We want to pack in as much as we can before it's over. That is my goal. At the end, I want to be able to smile and say, "That was one hell of a ride." When I get to the gates, I'll ask St. Pete, "Can I have a Mulligan?" or as my granddaughter used to say, "Do a din, Do a din." He'll just laugh, but he knows . . .

## Frame of Mind

Mondays used to be my worst day of the week, but that has changed. For those who believe that way, well, guess what, you will have a miserable day, too bad. Face it, you have a CHOICE, be miserable or MAKE IT GREAT!!! It's up to you. You know my choice.

## Changes

In my life, there has been a ton of changes that made me look at things differently. I realized that each day is a day of celebration. We have the opportunity to LIVE IT AND LOVE IT. When I read the obituaries each morning, I pray they all can say they did it right. That answer will never be known, but we have an opportunity to change our life with a simple "I CAN DO IT." Come on, the hardest part is taking that first step. The rest is easy. If you need help figuring out how, let me know.

## Life

During a discussion with a very good friend of mine, the subject of attitudes came up. We talked about how the environment, economy, tensions, stresses, etc. and how it effects people. I thought that what everyone needs is a good shot of L.I.F.E.

L-Live
I-It
F-Fully
E-Everyday

If taken daily, things will change. It took me a while, but it changed my life.

## Be Careful

You have heard the saying "Never fly off the handle, for you may wind up in the soup." If we become aggravated and want to speak our mind, just remember it is not easy to take back once something is said or to stop talking when we should. Training yourself to restrain is also not an easy task.

When the feeling gives you the need to open your mouth, THINK about what you are going to say, and whom it is going to effect. The result gives us no hard feelings, respect, and good tasting soup.

## Clarity

There comes a time in our lives that we see all things with the utmost clarity. Suddenly, everything that was affecting us has a pathway to the answers. It is almost a surreal experience. Suddenly, it all makes sense; hard questions are answered, and everything is as clear as never before.

This is when we make the right decisions. We are provided the answers for which we prayed so hard. We give thanks and are humbled with gladness.

## Life's Ups & Downs

Life is like a huge roller coaster with its many ups and downs. It is not the amount or depth of those swings that we encounter; it is how we experience each of them as memories to shape our biography in the end. It can either be a book of terror with the screaming, fear, worry . . . or a book on excitement with the fun, laughter, intrigue, love . . . From here on out, the pages are empty, and we are the author. Write your own adventure story. It is all in your hands.

## Day Light

As days get longer and the nights get shorter, leaves more day light time to enjoy the beauty of what God has given us. Take that extra minute of each day to love, smile, enjoy, share, hug, smell, touch, feel, give . . .

## MONDAY

MONDAY! There is nothing we can do to change it. No matter what we have facing us or what is scheduled to happen or the events we have no control over, we are confronted with the reality that MONDAY IS GOING TO HAPPEN.

Well, my friends, I have a few suggestions. Love every single minute of it; experience everything you can; embrace those close to you; and tonight, you will feel exhausted, but a hell of a lot happier.

## The Day's First Step

Every morning it starts out with that "First Step," lying in bed wondering what it will be like. That moment of hesitation is upon us, and our mind is clearing out the cobwebs and is beginning to focus on what lays ahead. It is THE decision of the day. Once the first foot hits the floor, it is all over, and reality rushes in with the sight of daylight, the first stretch, smell of coffee, loved ones all around . . . who is better than this. It is going to be a GREAT DAY.

## Adversity

Adversity is one of those things that we all face at some point in our lives, some of us more often than others are. We have to face it with conviction and determination, no matter what or who tells us differently. It is up to us. Sometimes, the outcome may not be in our control, BUT how we deal with it is. If taken with a "CAN DO" attitude, success is more probable than not.

## Friendship

Friendships are the most valuable gifts we have in our lives. They can take advantage of us, use us, complain to us, cry to us, scream at us, call us names in frustration, hug us, kiss us, and downright love us. All of this, knowing we can do the same with them if necessary, and they will be there. We all share the same bond. Cherish them with love and tenderness because they may be the only thing we have left in the end.

## Never Dull

Life is one event after another, and the greatest part about this is each event is different from the last. There is never a dull moment, unless you make it that way. Liven up your life because you only have one chance to do it right.

## Grandparent's Blessings

Grandchildren are a blessing. I never realized how much joy they bring to us as grandparents. It is exciting to see their growth, the excited look when they see you, the funny things they say or ask, the angelic looks on their faces, the playful times, hearing them laugh, the quiet times, snuggling times, the bone crushing hugs when they leave, and the empty feeling after they are gone. A grandparent's love is larger than life itself. I would not trade this job for anything in the world.

## Appreciation

I have experienced meeting many people, introduced to many cultures, foods, sights, and things in my past, but these only make me appreciate what I have and whom I love so much more. They also provided opportunities of which I would have never dreamed. The one thing that stands out among everything else is the love and hugs I received when I arrived home. NOTHING is more welcoming than LOVE.

## Listening

Listening to others could give us three things. First, we may learn something that we didn't know (knowledge). Second, we may learn something about the person we never knew (friendship). Third, we may find the person we have been looking for (love). It may pay to keep our mouths shut occasionally and open our ears and hearts.

## Time

Time is one of those things that can quickly slip past us unknowingly. Sometimes we get so engrossed in what we are doing, that, when we realize it, the time is gone. Setting personal priorities is important, but they should include not only spouses but also our children, pets, or ourselves. These are the things NOT to pass over because of lost time. MAKE the time happen, if not now, soon. If you don't, you will regret it. I know!!!

## The Market

I was at the local market recently checking out. The registers were full, so I lined up behind an elderly woman who was purchasing just a few items. The cashier presented the final total to her. She was shocked at the amount and wanted to know how much each item costs. Her challenges were mute, so the bottom line was the bottom line. While all of this was going on, I listened to the people behind me, heavy breathing, and sounds of discussed, complaining about how this "old person" was holding things up. Being the very controlled person I am, I reminded them that I was approaching this age and, God willing, they will too. There was silence among the crowd.

## Eye Sight

Every day we open our eyes and see the beauty of the day, sunrise, flowers, smiles, spouses, children, parents, coffee, food, car, etc. It does not make any difference what we see, BUT that we see.

My aunt had diabetes and lost her eyesight and mobility early in her years, and a good college friend had not been able to see since birth. Both were very functional, but they both could see how this limited their ability to do things that we normally take for granted.

So when you open your eyes every morning, be thankful that you can see the beauty that God created for us. Enjoy it and relish in it. HOWEVER, help others to see it through your eyes.

## Awkward Moment

What was your most embarrassing moment? I was about 15 years old and at a dance. I dressed up in a sport coat, white shirt, and tie. I was going with the girl of my dreams. Everything was perfect until I went to the rest room and found that my zipper was down all night long. My date told me that she did not want to embarrass me. I would have preferred to know earlier. We all had a great laugh over it, but having over a hundred people know, it was embarrassing. Now, I always check to make sure things are secured. (Yes, we are all human.)

## Human Race

Having traveled most of my corporate career, I became an avid people watcher, so any chance I have, I love seeing people in their natural environment. Everybody is different, in not only dress, but also in mannerisms, shapes, sizes, features, color, let alone the mental and internal differences.

For many years, airports were almost my second home, so people became a part of my family, in a way. The unique thing about people is, when placed in a public setting, some perform as if no one was watching. Others would be able to make "Candid Camera" a hit show again and yet more could create a new soap opera.

Bottom line is, God made each of us different for many reasons. One might be to make sure we don't become boring to each other, and the other, to provide us with the wonder of His being the ultimate Creator.

## Saturday Night

A long time ago, there was a song titled "Saturday Night is the Loneliest Night of the Week." We played it when I was in Drum Corps. Since I met my wife, there has never been a lonely night since. I am so thankful for her.

## Sundays

Sunday is a great day to give thanks.

We should give thanks for all we have, for the past week and our ability to arrive today alive, well, and in one piece (for some this is an accomplishment).

We should also give thanks for the freedom we have and being able to enjoy it every day.

We should also give thanks for the people who place their lives in jeopardy to give us our freedom, for those who have lost their lives for our freedom, and for those who are finally home from fighting for our freedom.

We should also give thanks and love to the families of the soldiers who are enduring life without their loved ones, and ask to give them strength to overcome the worry about their safety. We also pray for their safe and healthy return.

Sunday is a great day to give thanks . . . and again why not tomorrow.

## Hearing Protection

The older I get, the more sensitive my hearing is to noisy environments. When I go to indoor events, I need to wear earplugs. I love being with family, the kids, and grandkids. I love seeing and hearing them laugh, play, scream, and just being themselves. After spending the majority of my corporate career specializing in hearing protection, I want to continue to do this, so I protect what hearing I have left as much as possible. I hope others will understand it is not about them. It is personal for me.

## Mondays

Monday, huh? There is not a damn thing we can do to change that day. Every Monday morning, we have a decision to make. Either we can choose to be miserable and mope around all day, OR we can be cheerful, smiling, and laughing all day and bug the living hell out everyone else. I know which one I choose.

## Our Life

What is the first thing that runs through your mind when your eyes open in the morning? Is it, "What the hell am I going to face today?" Maybe, "Today is going to be a real bitch!" How about, "WTF is going to happen to me over the next 8 hours?" Or, "Is it 5 yet?" If you answered yes to any of the above, you might want to consider a readjustment. I remember these thoughts ever too well. It was the turning point of my life to change things around. I made plans to make things better for my life and me. It can be done, so IT IS UP TO YOU.

## Created Equal

Every day is a new day. It gives me a chance to start fresh, a clean slate to reflect on who I am and what I stand for. I believe in treating people with respect, no matter what their status is. I would say hello to the President with the same tone of voice as I would someone who is in need of help who has nothing to their name. Status means nothing to me. If you are a millionaire or you are someone who is having difficult times, you both deserve love and understanding.

The "Been there, done that" thing set a point in my life that will be with me for a long time. ANYONE who thinks they are better than anyone else is, talk to me first before opening your mouth.

## The Finger

I have determined that the finger is one of the most powerful instruments in the world. It can communicate that we are number one, need to go to the restroom, giving directions, telling someone how we "feel", giving the peace sign, informing someone where to sit, start a car, or do what I am doing now.

The one thing that I feel is the most horrible use of this important digit is POINTING AT SOMEONE in blame. Too many people use this as a means of discrediting others. It can either be a physical, verbal, or emotional pointing. This type of pointing is the most degrading, discriminating, discrediting, and devastating gesture there is.

Before you say anything, make sure it does not have a finger in it. I can say I use my finger everyday but mostly for typing, painting, sketching, carving, cooking, cleaning, etc. none of which is devastating to anyone. If we all pointed our finger praising someone, this would be a better place and fewer conflicts.

## Break Time

Do you ever experience a strange phenomenon during your day when a wave of peace just settles inside? It happened to me more when I was working in the corporate world, but it is that overwhelming moment of "Nothingness" that causes me to stop and smile.

I am not a psychologist, psychiatrist, or a therapist, so I have no idea what the technical term is. I just call it my "break time." It is the most peaceful feeling. It can last for a few minutes or sometimes seconds, but the main point is, it helps me to refocus on what is important. When "break" is over, life goes on.

Life is too short to let day-to-day junk wrap us up. Every once in a while stop and unload, readjust, or throw away the crap to allow us to enjoy today.

## Friendship

When we have not seen a friend in a long time and finally get together, that long gap never existed. It was as if we only talked yesterday. THAT is a friendship worth cherishing. It is as Aristotle once wrote, "A friend is a single soul shared by two people." Thank God for these special people in our lives.

## Saturdays

Saturday is a great day to spend chasing with the kids, shopping for the last minute "stuff" for Easter, setting things up for the dinner and guests, making sure the final touches are ready, and finally COLLAPSE. While we are going through all of this, PLEASE keep in mind, enjoy it, and love it. Family and friends are the reason why we are doing it to begin with. If you're not, just enjoy it anyway.

## Kindness

While out walking last week, I noticed how many people smile and say, "hello" or "How are you" or "Have a nice day," but, if you see these same people in their car . . .

Kindness is something that should be expressed openly no matter where we are, what we are doing, or whom we are with. It is a form of love that needs to be shown to others all the time. This world would be a better place if we could just show a little more kindness.

## Making Memories

Any time there is a reason to gather with loved ones, it is a time to absorb the memories into our heart and store them for a lifetime. It is a moment that we cannot relive except in our minds. Enjoy and love this day to the fullest.

## Trust

Other than love, TRUST is a very fragile thing because it is easy to place it in others, just as easy to have it destroyed, and it takes a lifetime to rebuild.

## Searching for Love

There was a time when I thought I would never again find love in my life. No matter what I tried or how hard I looked, the connective spark was not there. That was the problem. No matter how much effort I put in trying to find the "right one," or how hard I tried to impress others, the result was frustration.

It was not until I finally stopped putting so much effort in my search and started living my life to be happy and enjoy what I had, when that person knocked me off my feet. My lady did that over 15 years ago, and I thought I was doomed to be alone. Patience, mindset, and openness are the key. IT WILL HAPPEN!!!

## Simple Things

Sometimes the simplest things can bring us the greatest joy. It can be something like finding a penny (heads up, of course), reading your horoscope, finding a word in a crossword puzzle or word search, a kiss good morning or good night, a touch on the shoulder, finding a note of love, holding hands, hearing from a distant friend or loved one, reading a good joke, winning a game (Angry Birds???), a hug from your child or grandchild, hearing "I love you", or just a simple smile. They all count and can brighten someone's day. Share a little something simple of yourself today and brighten someone's day and your own day too.

## Feeling Down?

When I get down and feel lonely or sad (yes, it does happen), there is a routine I do that perks me up. First, I make a list of all the things that are bothering me, and then I start another list of my blessing and things for which I am thankful. The size of the second list outshines my problem list. By the time I stop writing, I feel that the problems I had were insignificant and can be easily solved.

It is amazing how our abundance grows, changes, resized, refashions, etc., but in the end, they are ours, which no one can take away. Be thankful for them and cherish them with all the energy you have.

## Thursdays

Thursday is always a fun day. It is not quite EOW (End Of Week) time to celebrate, but it can be a day of mischief. You know, getting antsy for TGIF to jump with joy. Kind of like a little kid going to the candy store only to find it closed and won't open for another 24 hours. The excitement, anticipation, heart beating, wide eyed, nose up against the window kind of excitement . . . ENJOY TODAY for tomorrow the store opens. By the way, the owner is going to be pissed because he has to wash the window now.

## Half True

I hate it when I hear people make statements that are "true," and, then find out it is partly true. For example, "I got paid today and made the bank deposit." Well, the check was $500, but the deposit was $50. Partial truth, it was deposited. Full truth, not all of it was deposited. Elections are won; people get married; friendships are ruined; people are imprisoned; good people are slandered all based on partial truths. If the whole truth is not appealing to the audience, why do we have to edit it out to make it more than it really is?

## No Regrets

Life is too short not to enjoy the time we have. My parents, God love them, worked as hard as anyone I know. They owned a tavern and had a good business for many years. They worked seven days a week, almost 24 hours a day. They loved what they did. Yet, spending all that time at work, they never neglected my sister and me

Many years later, I asked them if they regretted working so hard. Simultaneously, they said NO. Admiration for them abounds in our hearts. I could write a book about them alone. Now that is what I consider enjoying what you do.

## Blessings

For some, it is not easy to give, and for others, it is not easy to receive, yet for more, it is not easy to do either. It is a blessing for those who do both with happiness. Reaching deep inside, which category are you?

## Stress Relief

If there ever comes a time that we feel our stress gets to a point we can't or shouldn't go on, use the following steps to relieve that feeling:

Walk barefoot in the grass
Squish our toes in the sand
Chase the waves
Feed the birds
Watch butterflies
Throw a water balloon
Splash our feet in a puddle
Laugh until it hurts
Blow bubbles
Hold hands
And so on and on and on

Then it is time we have to evaluate our priorities and determine if we are missing the fun and simple things in life that make us live it rather than survive it. We need to find that "kid" that once was and bring us back to life. It is never too late.

## Patience

If there were one thing that is lacking in this world, it would be PATIENCE. We see it every day from sunrise to sunrise. Let's start with the first cup of coffee. If it is not ready ON TIME for any reason, I am sure we are not loving, kind, and courteous. If the children are at each other from the time they get up, how is your temperament? How about the "To-Do" list? We know that it cannot be done in one day, but we are going to try anyway, God forbid any one stand in our way.

I can go on forever with examples on how we have very little patience. Stop and think about what we are doing to others and ourselves. Let's try to make this NATIONAL PATIENCE DAY and make a change. Maybe it will become a part of us. Remember, all major adjustments in life begin with us.

## Thanks

Every day, I see and hear from my friends who appreciate the thoughts that I post. I cannot tell you how much it means to me to know that you are out there putting up with my babblings. I will honestly say that what I write are literally pop ups in this brain (heart powered) of mine based on previous experiences, encounters, and confrontations de jour. I cannot thank you enough for being loyal, appreciative, and, most of all, loving. You are my friends and will always hold a special place in my heart and prayers.

## The Whole Truth

Something stands out when I watch the evening news, the need to over embellish the reports. It concerns me about how this can sway someone's thoughts. I heard one last night that could convince one to vote for the opposition, BUT the report was only "partially" true. I am NOT a political person. In fact, I hate politics. Those friends, who are running for office, please make sure your statements are clean, fair, and honest. If this is how you run your campaign, I probably will support you. Partial truths, slander of an opponent, or twisting the truth have no room in my support. Keep it clean.

## Friends

Friends are a dime a dozen, but good friends are hard to find. The regular friends will be there for you when it is convenient for them. They will call you when you fit into their schedule. They will cry with you only if it is something that touches them. They will hold your hand or hug you only if you are the opposite sex.

A good friend is someone who will not care why, when, where, or what is needed with no questions asked and will be there whenever you need them. On the other hand, you will be there for them 24/7. I hope you all have "good friends."

## Friday

HEY, IT IS FRIDAY!!!! It took all week to get here. For some of us, it is the TRUE end of the week, for others, it is not. In either case, it is a day to celebrate for many reasons.

#1 is we woke up this morning and able to get up.
#2, it is a day we can make things happen FOR US.
#3, Friday is always a day to dance.

As long as I can stand up, breath, and move around, I am going to dance like hell. Are you joining me?

## Family

When I was growing up, my parents instilled in us the importance of family. We had meals together every night. On weekends, we either had relatives over, or we were at their house, and it wasn't even a holiday (this was on not only the Italian side, but also the Swedish side). When someone was ill and hospitalized, the waiting room was filled with the whole family and no one left until the final diagnosis and prognosis were given. The family was the center of all living activities.

Times have changed. Now the total family only gets together on holidays and special occasions. Also due to the times, the immediate family isn't able to have dinner together because of prior commitments or work schedules or kids sporting events. The only thing I would like to encourage is gathering once a day or, at least, once a week to give thanks for the loved ones we have and show how much they mean to us. Maybe we can get back to the old values of putting family in the center again.

## Saturday

Interestingly enough it is Saturday. Let's live it until we are exhausted. Let's laugh so much our sides ache and tears are running down our cheeks. Let's hug each other so tight we lose our breath. Most importantly, let's tell each other how much we love them. Enjoy it until the last minute is up.

## Kids' Lives

It took me many years to realize how important my presence in my children's life was. A few moons ago, I spent a ton of my life on airplanes, in and out of airports, living out of suitcases, forgetting what hotel I was at, or even waking up not remembering what country I was in. The ONE thing I did remember was my children's activities, and how soon I could be home to see them.

I did everything I could to be there. The sacrifice of taking an overnight flight to be at the starting line of a track event, first tee of a golf tournament or push the speed limit for kickoff at a cheer squad performance was most important to me. I tried to attend as many events as possible, and I did it not only for them but also for me because I was proud to be a DAD and proud to be their father.

I don't know if they remember it. That makes no difference to me, but I will remember every one of them because I am the DAD. My children mean everything to me and always will. Now my grandchildren add to that pride. Love your children with everything you have. You will feel better for it, and they will too.

## Sunday

Sunday is a day meaning a lot to me. It is time to spend with our loved ones. Enjoy this special day because it was originally set up as a "DAY OF REST." For some, it was yesterday. Well, either case, let's do everything we can to just that, rest and enjoy

## Evaluate

There comes a time when we need to take a few minutes, step back, and evaluate ourselves. IF you do this properly, you should be amazed at what you find the accomplishments, the blessings, and the amount of graces that have accumulated. You can also count the loves in your life or the number of friends you have that you can depend on. If you can go through this list and feel you have everything, you will have a GREAT day. If not? You can still have a great day looking to how you can change your life to accumulate these gifts. They mean more than your paycheck, your investments, or your job status. All of these things can vanish in a flash. The others last a lifetime. EVALUATE.

## Monday

Well, look here, it's MONDAY. We are beginning a fresh new week. Let's start it out with a smile on our faces, laughter in our hearts, being friendly to everyone, and put love in every word you speak. If you set a goal to bug the living hell out of everyone you meet with kindness and happiness, you will have a great day.

## Gatherings

Does everyone feel the confusion and chaos when groups of people gather? It is almost like the first day of school. It "feels" like meeting everyone for the first time, but you have known these people for ages. That time of absence from each other seemed to have wedged a distance between you and them and vice versa. The handshakes are tense, the hugs are weird, the smiles are frozen, but inside, you know some of these people better than you know yourself. That part of the gathering is the most stained.

When all formalities are over, everything finally falls into place and love prevails. It floods into everyone. Even the room seems lighter and happier. It doesn't hurt to let others know that you love them.

## Tuesday

Tuesday to me is a nothing day because the only time a Tuesday is celebrated is when Holidays, New Years, or the 4th of July land of a Tuesday. Fat Tuesday does, you can officially celebrate it only if you live in New Orleans. There are pseudo-celebrations, but they do not count. I am officially declaring Tuesday as TIGHT Tuesday, only because it is not the beginning of the week, far from the end of the week, and is stuck in between the start and middle of the week. That is tight. Now every day of the week has a "special" significance. HAPPY TIGHT TUESDAY, ENJOY!!! (Just don't tell Hallmark®)

## Excuse Me

"Excuse me" are two simple words that go a long way. When you bump into someone on the bus or subway, a simple excuse me takes care of the situation. How about standing in line for something as simple as a DRIVER'S LICENSE RENEWAL, you accidentally bump into the person in front of you. You simply say, excuse me, and everything is fine. Sitting in a restaurant having dinner with your spouse, special friend, parents, boss or anyone who means a lot to you, and you burp (or pass anything else you might be embarrassed about), a simple excuse me might not cover all the embarrassment, but is a good start. A little courtesy goes a long way.

## Intelligence

There is one thing that I truly admire in people, humility. For example, some people are probably more intelligent than anyone in a room is but don't show it. They also are mature enough to have everyone around them feel comfortable where they can say anything without fear of embarrassment. That to me is the sign of an intelligent people.

Most of the time it is best to say nothing, than to say something and confirm to everyone that we are . . .

## God's Gifts

Have you ever sat back and admired the wonderful things that He has provided us? The beauty of a simple flower, the serenity of the ocean, the breathtaking sight of cloud formations, the sound of birds singing, warmth of the sun, and the coolness of a breeze are all wonderful things that have been provided for us to enjoy. When was the last time you stopped and took notice of these gifts? If you haven't, plan on it soon. Life is too short to let them slip away.

## The Friday Dance

Once visiting our grandchildren in the Midwest on a Friday, we were sitting having a cup of coffee and the two of them came into the kitchen twirling around and slapping their hands singing, "IT'S FRIDAY; IT'S FRIDAY; IT'S FRIDAY." We learned this craziness was a routine started to celebrate the upcoming weekend. It is called the "Friday Dance."

To carry on the newly formed family tradition, it is time to do the Friday dance. Kick up your heels, swing your partner around, and hug everyone you see. This will open many of peoples' thoughts. Either it will cause them to enjoy life, or it might shock the living hell out of them. Enjoy it in either case.

## The Wedding

A marriage is a formal union between two people expressing their love for each other. It is their commitment to one another for the rest of their lives in times of prosperity or adversity. Today, two of our loved ones will do just that, and all who will witness this great event are honored to partake in the festivities. The preparation, planning, and expense for this great day took months to develop and finalize. It will only take a few hours to execute. It will create a lifetime of memories filled with all the love the universe can hold, and be in our hearts forever. May God bless this beautiful couple.

## Family Gatherings

Whenever there is a chance for the family to gather, take advantage of the moment. We should celebrate this special time with enthusiasm and happiness. What we take with us at the end of the night are all the memories etched in our minds to last a lifetime. Holding close the love shared in our hearts and laughing about all the fun. This is what life is all about. There is not enough money in the world that can replace those moments.

## What Others Think . . .

I have concluded that there will always be people who:

. . . don't like what I have to say
. . . tell me that they hate my looks
. . . despise my positive attitude
. . . don't agree with my outlook on love, life or both
. . . don't understand my religious beliefs
. . . are disturbed with my hair cut or something

Bottom line is, how they feel about me is their problem, not mine. People have been trying to change me, adjust me, or tell me how I should live my life. Well, my friends, I tried to fit in with the "cool" people, seek friendships with the right people, and tried to change to be considered acceptable. The only thing this taught me is I am no one else, but me. If you don't like it, well, it's your loss, because I am a great guy and so are you.

## Please

When I was in the market the other day, I overheard a conversation between a child and her mother. The child, about 4 years old, was wanting something from the counter display, but only said, "Mommy, I want that . . ." The mother calmly said, "No." The child proceeded to yell, "I want that. I want that, I want that." The mother looked at her with a face that would have dropped her in her tracks.

The little girl stopped yelling, stared at her mother, and asked in the sweetest little voice and the cutest face, "Mommy, may I please have that?" The mother picked her up, hugged her, kissed her, and gave her the prize. It was only a flavored Chap Stick. A little "PLEASE" goes a long way even for a little girl. Let's not lose touch with manners.

## Growing U

It seems like my thoughts are provoked when I am shopping. I was in the checkout line and had the opportunity to have two people in front of me talking about their neighbor who allows their children to play outside after dinner and how disruptive this is to their TV shows.

When I was a kid, we played outside until sundown, even on school days if the homework done. During summer vacation, we stayed out until someone called for us, and I have no recollection as to what time that was.

This was where imaginations were born. I know there is now a lot of fear about this, but, if it is in an area where it is safe, let the kids play. I would give anything to play Kick the Can, Hide and Seek, or Tag, again. I would need an EMT afterwards, but it would be fun.

## Highway Love

Making the trip to Virginia Beach last week for our niece's wedding, we encountered many different types of drivers. There was the "Speedster," who travels about 100 mph to get ahead of everyone, only to be passed up when he is pulled over by the police. Then there is the "Jumper," who tries to get ahead of everyone before merging into one lane for construction. Have you ever heard about the "Lane Hopper"? When there is traffic congestion, this is the guy who hops from one lane to another thinking he is going to get farther ahead than anyone else does, and probably, in the end, he is only a car or two ahead once traffic picks up. The "Race to the Exit" guy is the one who gives me heart attack. He is racing along in lane 3 and needs to cut in front of everyone to get to the exit.

I probably could go on, but the point is, there were millions of people out driving, and all it would have taken was one little mistake and many might not have made it home and some possibly did not. Drive safely. The happiness of your family depends on it.

## Road Trip

When I was growing up in the Midwest, nice beaches were non-existent close to home like in Rhode Island. It was a 50-mile trip to the nicest one in Lake Geneva, and 70 miles to Lake Michigan. In either case, it was a road trip. We made the most of it.

We asked friends, aunts, uncles, cousins, friends of friends, etc. and try to get as many people to go to make it a major event and not just a trip to the lake. It would mean packing lunches, snacks, drinks, change of clothes, additional swimming suits, just in case. It would start at 8 AM and go until sundown with a caravan going in each direction. We were exhausted when we arrived home.

The whole idea was not only family time but also community time. Those who started the day not knowing everyone in the group became best friend at the end of the day. There is very little of this going on this day and age. Let's get back to getting to know our neighbor and including them in our everyday life, even if it is just going to the beach.

## The Sun

I had a thought after our evening walk and watching the clouds getting brighter in hopes the sun will FINALLY appear after days of cloudy weather. It is amazed at how much we rely on the sun to help us with our dispositions. The longer the clouds guard us from the sun, the more we are apt to be irritable, short-tempered, unsettled, sluggish, non-energetic, lethargic, and blah, blah, blah. Just like anything else, we should not allow anything or anyone control our emotions or ourselves except for us. Well, it may not control us, but that damn sun sure as hell is a kick in the ass when it is emotionally needed. Enjoy it, every minute of it.

## Do Over's

IF you had one thing in your life that you could do over again, what would it be? Would you do something different like correct a problem you had or maybe a decision you always questioned or relive a moment that meant so much to you?

Personally, I wouldn't change a thing in my life. The mistakes I made, the wrong decisions, the precious moments are all what made me who I am today, and I kind of like whom I am and wouldn't change a thing.

## Good Friends

You inherit your family, but you choose your friends. Choose those who will stay with you under any circumstances, and you would do anything for them, anywhere, anytime. Fortunately, I am blessed with some of the greatest friends and family in the world. God bless them all.

## Morning Decisions

Waking up each morning with the attitude that this day is going to be one of the greatest in my life is just as easy as waking up feeling that today is going to bring nothing but grief. If I choose the first, anything that happens good or bad can be accepted, but if I choose the second, I have to wait for something good to happen to make it better. Why start the day waiting when you can have it immediately?

## Believe

It took me many years to figure it out. If I didn't believe in myself, no one else would either. This epiphany came after many bumps and bruises early in my career. Once I learned this, no one could take it away, and life became more enjoyable.

## Depression

I have to confess, I do have periods when I am down, depressed, miserable, wanting to be alone, and sad. I deserve to feel like this occasionally. I heard it's healthy. I also know I am the only one who has the right to kick my butt to get out of this funk and put me on the path of happiness. If I had to depend on others to do this, I would never be happy. I only look to others to feed on their positivity. This is called helping each other; novel thought, huh?

## "The Crisis"

I know people who live their lives in crisis mode. Everything is paramount to their own or everyone else's existence. When I listen to the situation or the problem, I find it is only a "mole hill" and not the "mountain" as originally portrayed, and easily resolved or put into perspective. My concern is not so much the current crisis, but the result of this repeatedly happening to the point where no one will listen any more. So if a REAL crisis occurs, will anyone respond? It is not easy to change an old habit, I know, but it will help us live longer, happier, and have more friends.

## Mother's Day, 2012

There was someone who was there from the beginning, soothing our hurts and pains, hugging us when we were down, kissing us for no reason what so ever, scolding us for doing wrong, worrying about us when we were on our own, laughing with us when we did something crazy, crying with us when we were wronged, shedding tears of joy when we did something grand, and stood by us during the tough times. This person was always there showing us what love is, teaching us how to love, and never asking for anything in return. We love you Mom.

## Surprise

Hearing from someone who you haven't talked to in months, is a lift for spirits that cannot be matched. Even though the call lasted a few minutes, it was great just to know they were thinking about you enough to make that effort. If you have not talked to anyone in a while, give them a call. It may come at a time when they needed it the most. Spread that love.

## Follow Your Passion

When I was in high school, there was bullying, but it took the form of ignoring you as opposed to mental or physical abuse. I was not a star or famous or popular or well known or . . . As a matter of fact, I might have been considered a "Nerd" because I was in Drum Corps which was not too well known back then and not school affiliated.

I lived everyday to perform and march with my fellow musicians on weekends, plus one night a week, and all summer long. I did and pursued what I loved. I felt successful at it.

I never made it to be prom or homecoming king, valedictorian, number one jock, etc. I followed my dream and accomplished what I felt was my number one love. THAT was important to me and will always be held close to my heart. Not only do I live the memories of my experiences, but I also learned to love music and meet people from all over the country at a very young age. I will never regret being different for the experience, I gained. Never pass up and opportunity to do what you love. Succeed or fail, I tried it and loved every minute.

## Old Style

When I was growing up, video games consisted of trying to get the rabbit ears on the TV to bring in a clear picture, and the one who succeeded was the winner. Writing a quick note on a piece of paper and passing it through 4-5 people to get to the right person was our form of texting. Photos of the things going on in school were taken by professional photographers or someone from the journalism class, but took one to three weeks to get the prints published. TV shows were shown on three network channels, not 500 different ones.

I am not saying that progress is wrong, but I am saying it should not take away the values of family, intelligence, or creativity. Sometimes the simplest things are the greatest things on earth. It just takes a little sacrifice, thought, and love. Try it sometime. You might be surprised at what you find.

## Technology Choices

Life can be simpler than you think. I write about the "old" days when things were not as hectic as they are today. Now, we have options that we did not have back then, but these options come with choices, Yes or No or Sometimes.

We can choose Yes to jump into the tech world and text all day, phone all day, schedule ourselves to the minute, and wind ourselves up tight as a drum.

We can choose NO to ignore the advances in technology, live in the past, and let the present exist without us, thus losing touch with everyone.

We can choose Sometimes and have a happy combination of both worlds, staying in touch with everything going on, but have down time to give us some breathing room. I am a Sometimes person. I enjoy the technology, but it will not control my time, thoughts, or attitude.

## Politics

I wrote this yesterday as a response to a reader asking for my political opinion.

I am not into politics at all. In fact, I try to bury my head in the sand until it is time to make a decision. My thought is that no matter what office or position is being sought, the views and plans of that person changes so many times from the time they say, "I'm running" to the day of election. I find it best to take the last statements made before heading to the polls and go with that. Face it, Satan is a politician. He promised Adam and Eve everything; they followed him and we all know where it got them.

## Old Indian Proverb

An old Indian Proverb says, "When you were born, you cried and the world rejoiced. Live your life in such a way so that when you die, the world cries and you rejoice."

Is not it amazing how the path leading to a full life turns things completely around? Live your life to the fullest, my friends. You only have one. Work hard. Work smart. Have fun. In the end you can say, "Yup, I've had a hell of a ride," and rejoicing all the way.

## College Poem

I found this in the Bovi Archives of written nonsense.

Yahoo!, Never fear,
For Monday is here,
So bring with it great cheer,
And end it with a beer.

Sorry, this is a college thing. I usually enjoyed my days.

## Please Give

There are so many "Awareness" organizations out there, all of which are great causes. I wish we could donate to all of them, but financially, some of us cannot. What we all can do is give our prayers and support as much as we can to all of them. There is not one cause that we do not know someone who may be affected in one way or another. Give if we can, but we can all offer a prayer of hope and love.

## Silence

There are times when I need to keep my mouth shut and times when I should verbalize my thoughts. The other day I was at the market and overheard a husband (I think) complaining to his wife about all of the things he had to do in the house, and there was no time for him to do the things that he wants to do. The more I listened, the more upset I got.

First, I did not know their circumstances at home, but the look of embarrassment on the wife's face was enough to give me a hint. I told the husband that this is not the place to tell everyone about his home life. No one cares to hear his problems. Furthermore, we have enough problems of our own without adding his.

The stunned look on his face was worth the price of admission, and there was not another word spoken. Thank God for his restraint for I was able to walk out of there without physical harm. I vowed AGAIN to keep my mouth shut. (We all know that will never happen).

## Memorial Day

Today we commemorate the people who have given their lives in either present or past wars defending our freedom and peaceful way of life. We want to say thank you for your sacrifice of time, hard work, and in some cases your life for us. We also pray for your families in gratitude for their strength during those times of your absence. We also give our sincere sympathy for those who have lost their loved one fighting for us. This is for TODAY AND ALWAYS.

## Breaking Point

We all have times of reflection, examination, and evaluation. We look deep within our being to find that point that is driving us nuts to reach some faction of sanity. When the frustration point is finally achieved, we realize the best approach is to "Just Go with it."

## Money

Is it not amazing what money does to us? We lose sleep if we do not have enough. We worry when we have enough or too much. Most people think that having money is less worrisome than not having any. In my life, I have seen both sides of this scenario, and I think neither side has an advantage. If I did not have enough, I focused on what to do with whatever I had. If I had enough, I focused on how it can help others. Being resourceful, resilient, and helping others will always attract prosperity to us. It works every time.

## Life

Faith: knowing that something will happen.
Hope: waiting for it to happen.
Love: it happened.
No wonder the greatest of these is LOVE.

## Winners

My wife and I were at the market last night. When we were checking out, I was talking to the bagger who told us he participated in the Special Olympics and won two Gold Medals. His pride was beyond anything I have ever seen. Winning the lottery would not have been as rewarding for him as this. This touched me to realize everyone has their peak points in life. He accomplished something great for himself. What is yours?

## Personal Inventory

How thankful are you for what you have? Take an inventory, write it down, there is no limit of how many items you list, list only positive points, and make them all capital letters. When you feel you are finished, take a few minutes, walk around, and see if there is anything missing. Look deep inside to find anymore additions for the list and add those.

Now sit and read it, memorize it, and engrave it to your mind. Let it burnish a mark in your stone of life. This way you will always know the reasons you want to love life.

## Sunday

Sunday is a good day to give thanks for all of our blessings. It is also a good day to spend it with family or friends. When growing up, the Swedish and Italian sides of my family loved gathering on Sundays for good food, lots of playing, and tons of love, so enjoy yours!!!

## Self Reflection

When I get up in the morning, I look myself in the mirror. Today, I can smile, but there was a time when I did not like what I saw. It took facing reality, making decisions that I never thought possible, changing attitudes, and looking DEEP inside to clean house. It was not an easy task to face alone, but that journey allows me to be ME. That is most important and not all of the material bullshit and phony facades. You should try it too.

## Geek

When I was growing up, I may have been different. I think they called us weirdoes, who became nerds, which evolved to geeks, and I have no idea what the title is today. For some, it was a stigma and for others it was just a way of life. The titles do not matter. As we matured, those times gave us the strength to be ourselves, to grow as an individual, and see others differently. Funniest thing, I never remember being alone or isolated.

## Happiness

You can have all you want in this life, the riches, cars, big houses, job, position, land, "friends," popularity, clothes, beautiful things, etc.

HOWEVER, in the end, all you have left is you. Can you be happy with that?

## Bad Day Remedy

May the weather or grump people dampen or hinder your day. If it starts to get to you, just close your eyes, click your heels three times, and say, "There's no place like home." Then, BINGO, there is no more Lion, Tin Man, or Scarecrow to bother you.

## Having Fun

The phrase that makes me cringe is, "What would people think?" I know we all heard that statement since childhood at one time or another. This was our parents' way of telling us not to do something that would cause them embarrassment. This has stuck in my mind for many years. Now, in my mid-sixties, I get told this when I walk into Toys R Us and start all the toys singing or playing music or tooting horns, or skipping down the middle of the aisles. Well, this may be embarrassing, but I only live once and having fun can be embarrassing at times. Isn't that what living it to the fullest means?

## Growing Up

Here is a phrase that gets to me, "Oh, grow up!" Well, I have spent the majority of my 60 plus years trying to grow up, but every time I start thinking of this, I recall a song from the original "Peter Pan" with Mary Martin, "I won't grow up." Case closed!!!

## Smile

When my wife and I were at the market one night checking out, the bagger was a young man about high school age. He was conversing with us as we were standing there, and, me being me, I made the statement of "Keep smiling." He come back refreshed me with "I try to smile all day. It helps when I am down, and it helps others. It makes the day go faster." That was refreshing to hear such words of wisdom from someone so young. I wish he could rub off on a few others.

## Father's Day 2012

Today should be a good day for us to give thanks. Not only be thankful for all the fathers in the world, but also for the fathers who are no longer a part of this world. In either case, they will always hold a place of high honor in our hearts. A saying I read this morning rather says it all. "Anyone can be a Father, but only special ones can be called Daddy." Happy Father's Day to my friends out there even the ones who hold both titles. God bless you all. Enjoy the day!

## Mornings

Waking up in the morning listening to the birds chirping as the sun rises; the day gets brighter almost by the minute; I feel a slight chill in the air and snuggle under the covers. A huge smile comes to my face because of that peaceful moment before the day begins. I avoid putting my feet on the floor for as long as possible because once I do, reality sets in . . .

## Love

There is only one thing that stands between you and true love, yourself. If your heart is ready to accept it, it will happen. It has to be open for it to enter. It cannot open when it is desperate. You can control desperation.

## Enthusiasm

I had once read that enthusiasm is the source of energy, which enables us to accomplish anything. Can you imagine harnessing that source of energy and use it to grow our love or relationship or marriage or family? This would be a better world with stronger people in it. It all begins with us, so pass it on.

## Our "Stuff"

Are you ever so wound up with all the "Stuff" in your life that you forget the important things? Like, reintroducing yourself to you, loving those who mean so much to you, reaching out to others in need, finding a way to expand your life for the good of others, or just being thankful for what you have. Life is way to short to not get rid of all the "Stuff," take the time, and look around to see all the glorious things in it.

## Sharing Love

I have to believe that love is something that does not run out. No matter where I am, what I am doing, whom I am with, or whom I am talking to, I always feel that love is all around. I have it when I wake up and carry it with me all day long. I share it often. I show it at any chance I get. I give it away to anyone who wants it and even to some who do not. You all have been recipients of my love at some point in time. Please do me a favor, share that love with others who you feel worthy, and to those I cannot reach. Thank you.

## Love

While on the subject of love, it is the strongest thing in the world. It can be received, given, or stolen. It can be stomped on, beaten down, or thrown out. It can be tucked away, hidden, or saved. HOWEVER, the most important thing is that it never leaves us. It is something that is always there, will never run out, and grows on a second to second basis. All it needs is a little attention. Pay attention to your love, and it will love you back ten times more.

## Plans

Have you taken time to find out what you want in life? I know we have all made plans at some point in our lives, set our objectives, laid out our timelines, reviewed them on a routine basis, revised them when necessary, and put them in action. Do any of these plans include the ones you particularly love? If you do not include them, these plans become meaningless or empty. Try to include them and let them become a part of your "life." You may find it all more meaningful.

## Time

Time is a fascinating element in life. Sometimes there is not enough of it, and, other times, it cannot move fast enough. The one constant is that it moves at its own speed, and the rate only exists in our minds usually based on what is happening at that moment. Talking to someone you are not fond of, time is stagnant. If you are with people you love, and every minute is precious, time goes by too fast. Make the right choices with the time you have.

## Make Time

Time is something that we hold so precious that it becomes monumental in our lives. Time becomes everything. We base our lives on time. We are either too late or too early. There is either too much of it or not enough of it. Our eating and sleeping habits center on time. We punch in and punch out on a time card. Are we going to make our flight on time? Deadlines to meet, meetings to attend, start times, end times, post times, etc. Time! The one thing that we should always do is MAKE time for ourselves, and those we love. That time is precious to us, and it will always be imprinted on our loved ones' minds for the rest of their lives. Now, tell me what deserves so much of your time.

## Politicians

I hate politics, especially during a major election year. Good friends, who are into this, completely change their personalities. Politicians, who 4 years ago were for something, are now against it because of the "party" focus. The amount of money spent to elect someone could be used to put a dent in our national debt or feed the hungry.

What would happen if each candidate had to raise their own money with no corporate donations, no Super Pac donations, only use their personal savings, and run on their own platform? I wonder if this would bring the candidates closer to the people, they serve. At times, I am not quite certain that they even realize who we are.

## Choices

One thing that thrills me more than anything is someone who recognizes that they have choices in their lives. To hear the lift in their voices, to see the TRUE smiles on their faces, the sound of happiness of knowing they have control, the actions they take, and the successes they have. These are more of a reward to me than winning a multi-million dollar lottery. Helping others is what makes life so great.

## Love

Love, that mystical emotion that draws us, captures us, makes us crazy at the same time ironically gives us sanity. Love causes us to lose everything, but then again it puts so much more into our lives. It can be a real drag on our style, but it also fires excitement and passion. Love is something that we don't want to have it control us, but it dominates our every moment. If you feel like you don't have it, look for it because it is there. If you know you have it, cherish it, and hold it close. If you feel like it is lost, have faith. It will show up ten times stronger. The most important element is BELIEVE.

## Be Yourself

You don't have to like doing everything your partner likes to do. In a way, that is boring. You can think alike in many ways, or maybe know what they might say in certain circumstances, but diversity in life is good. The challenge of this is knowing how to handle it or work with it. That is where, love, patience, and understanding comes in. The adventure is the differences each other brings to the party.

## Finding Love

This is for those who feel they may have lost love in their hearts. The feeling of loneliness, emptiness, withdrawal, desperation, even indifference toward themselves and others, and sometimes sheer anger out of jealousy are all common feelings they may experience.

Well, the good news is that you have not lost it. It is still inside of you. Love is something that we tend to shelf periodically, but it cannot be lost. It is up to us to relocate it and jumpstart it again. No one will hand it to you.

Like, the coach always told us in sports, "You have to want it in order to win it." Well, you have to want to locate it in order to feel it. Well, find your love inside and cherish it for the rest of your life. I did.

## Challenges

We all have experienced challenges in our lives, and some are more difficult than others are. Do not compare yours with anyone else because their circumstances or environment is completely different from yours. A suggestion would be to concentrate on your own. Those are more important than anything is.

## Uncertainty

Time is uncertain, so make sure to tell all those close to you how much you love them and, if close enough, hug them. Don't go through life wishing you had shown your love for them when it is too late to do anything about it.

## Beauty

When someone said that beauty is only in the eyes of the beholder, they were not wrong. One person might see something as beautiful, but someone else may not. I see beauty in a piece of barn wood where someone else sees scrap lumber. Respecting one another's opinions is important in almost anything, but what is more important is an "attempt" on our part to see it the way they do. It is not mandatory to acknowledge it; at least the heart is there.

## Ego

How's your ego lately? Is it big enough where it gets in the way of your life? Is it causing you to work your ass off to keep ahead of the next person? Is it getting in the way of your ability to say you are sorry? Are you stumbling over it making a fool of yourself? Maybe it is so big that you cannot tell someone how you feel.

Well, my friends throw that damn thing called ego out the window because it is ruining your life. Gain some self-respect and start loving life and others again.

## Letting Go

The scariest thing in life to do is to "let go." Think about it. When we were kids, we would hang from the monkey bars and the only way down was to "let go." Growing up, we fell in love, but it didn't work out, so we had to "let go." We went to college or the service or just had to leave home, so we had to "let go." We moved out of the parents' house for the final time, so now both our parents and we had to "let go." Our children grew up and started to drive, date, work, or just go out, we had to "let go." When we see them get married, we had to "let go." We live our lives fully and give our love, teach lessons, tell stories and build legacies, but in the end, now they have to "let go."

My friends live each day as if it were your last, hug anyone close to you, spread as much love as you can in every second of the day, and, most of all enjoy doing it and do not let go.

## Human Race

We were on vacation for a few days enjoying the relaxing time together and doing what we do best, people watching. The human race is an amazing species. If I were an alien, I would begin to wonder how this planet lasted as long as it did. Courtesy is not one of our greatest virtues. Patience only appears when it is someone else's benefit. Kindness shows up when there is no other choice.

People, please take under consideration how you would feel and act accordingly. If you want someone to slam a door in your face, block you from exiting the parking lot, or ignore something someone dropped, then go ahead and keep doing what you are doing. You have to live with yourself for a lifetime and try to get along with everyone else. It is your choice.

## The Boss

I used to have a boss who had a sign that said, "When entering this office, put your ego in the waste basket below, hold your head up high, and enter with dignity, BUT be willing to share." It created an atmosphere of togetherness and gave everyone power to share. I think he had it right.

## Sharing God

I see the postings in Facebook about God answering prayers. Some put time limits on sharing the post to get results. Some even put consequences on them if we ignore it. Some say there are bad things that will happen if we don't share them.

Well, my friends, our God does not base His decisions on Facebook, Twitter, You Tube, or any other type of social media to grant his graces. He does review what we publish, but that is not His determining factor. If you like the post, share it. If you don't like it, don't feel intimidated to the point that you will fear the chance of not waking up tomorrow morning. Let's be realistic!!!

## Whole Picture

We listen to the news every night, and there is one thing that really disturbs me. When a broadcaster reports that there is a problem with 200,000 of something and not state the total population, it is misleading information.

Is it out of 200,001(significant) or 200,000,000 (Uhh). The number sounds huge from one aspect, BUT it is insignificant from another. If they are going to state the facts, how about stating the total facts, so we can make an educated decision, this is another reason why I HATE POLITICS.

## Health Care Personnel

I had a procedure done on Wednesday, which called for an anesthetic. Well, the effects of this lasted two days. I couldn't put together a publishable or understandable thought. It was extremely unnerving for me.

I wanted to write about the nurses and aids that cared for their patients and their families. These professionals handle anything from a miserable person to one who is apprehensive and scared. In either case, they were there for us and did everything they could to make this experience as comfortable as possible. My admiration goes out to them.

## Complaints

Why do people complain so much? They talk about the heat, humidity, sun rising early, sun setting late, lousy service, long red lights, slow drivers, pot holes in the streets, no parking spaces closer, slow moving old people, loud or crying kids, no rain, too much rain, fast growing grass, work colleagues, dirty rest rooms, etc. I think I could make this list longer than the Constitution included all the amendments and proposed legislation.

Does anyone realize that "grumping" only pisses other people off? If there is nothing that can resolve this, shut up and deal with it. If a solution is possible, don't bitch and do something about it.

## Half-Year Review

This year is a little over half over. That means we have less than 6 months to have as much fun as possible. If you packed a ton of fun in the first 6 months, you have the next 6 months to see if you can do better. It is all a matter of putting your mind to it. You gotta love life.

## Attitude

Life is full of twists and turns, ups and downs, highs and lows, rough and smooth times, BUT it is all in the attitude and enthusiasm you approach it that directs the outcome. Begin each day with an attitude pep talk in the mirror, and your day will at least start great. Be enthusiastic in whatever you do, and that should carry you through it. Mostly, put your heart into it, and it will turn out great.

## Love

God made everyone capable of love. It is who or what we choose to love that makes the difference. The intensity of that love is also our choice, and this separates the lovers of people and the lovers of things. The lovers of things will only have things, but the lovers of people are the ones who will find happiness and riches of life.

## Reach Out

If you have not talked to someone you love lately, give them a call, and let them know you how you feel. It may brighten up their day and yours too.

## Giving

What better feeling is there in life than giving? You get to see the sparkle in their eyes, the huge smile on their faces, the surprised looks, the tears of happiness running down their cheeks, and the hugs and kisses of gratitude. All of this comes from one little moment of giving. If you have never experienced it, try it.

## Anger Management

How do you defuse anger within yourself? If you never get mad, you are not human. Physical and verbal abuses are not acceptable behaviors in any case and not ignored or taken lightly.

I am referring to the anger that happens when someone does something against your wishes. The old adage of counting to ten or one hundred, depending on the circumstances, helps. Walking away to cool off is not bad if the person does not follow. Maybe closing your eyes and thinking of pleasant things are all good or just work. What works for you? If you share that with someone, it may help them learn to cope with anger. Sharing is great.

## Positive Thinking

Have you ever tried to go a full day without saying a negative comment about anything or anyone? It is one of the hardest things to do. We have negativity drilled into us since birth, and it takes pure concentration and effort to think positively.

Being raised in the Catholic school system for nine years (in the 50's, no less), not only was there negativity, but also combining that with guilt. This was a lethal combination.

Let us focus and center ourselves today on nothing but positive statements, thoughts, and actions. I really would be interested in what the result is. You may be surprised.

## Honesty

Honesty is something that is the backbone to humanity. It can make you, break you, and help you succeed, destroy you, exonerate you, and even bury you. HOWEVER, it guarantees to bring peace, harmony, trust, wealth, friendship, peace of mind, but most of all love. Try it you may like it.

## Be Happy

No matter what the weather is on the outside, it should be sunny on the inside. Like the song said, "Don't worry, be happy." Smile it saves years on your life.

## Like Yourself

When you look yourself in the mirror, what do you see? If you like what you see, have a nice day. If you do not like what you see, look inside to find out why and change it. Life is too short to live with someone you do not like.

## Morning Thoughts

What is the first thing you do when you get up in the morning? Is it remembering that it is a day where there are tons of things to accomplish? How about a day that nothing needs to be accomplished resulting in a day of relaxation? Maybe we remember that it is a workday and have meetings scheduled all day. What about that list of errands that need finalizing to give us less stress? Does anyone give thanks for another beautiful day for living?

## Self-Help

Have you ever gotten so involved with something that it completely consumed you? It kept you away from your loved ones, your friends, your obligations, your health, etc. This is an indicator that it is time to REST, RELAX, REGENERATE. Remember, you come first in your life, so take care of you first.

## Love

Love each other so much today that it overwhelms you both and spills over onto others.

## Talents

Have you been creative lately determining how you can use your talents to help others? It occurred to me that we all have things we can do which are our own. Have you given any thought as to how you can use those to make a difference in other peoples' lives? These are things you can share, not cost a dime, be creative at the same time, and make others happy.

## Happiness

There was a time in my life when I was over taken with the material things, the social status, the "right" people, and I could go on forever. I was so wound up in it that I lost perspective of what was important. It took me a while to understand what had happened, set a plan for adjustment, and finally make changes in my life. Happiness cannot be purchased or received from others. It can only come from within. That is permanent and true happiness.

## Life's Lessons

I have made many mistakes in my years. I only regret is any sadness I may have caused to anyone by those mistakes, but I will always take with me the lessons I learned from them, the experience I gained from them, and the person I had become because of them. There is nothing more humbling than to correct a wrong, but, in my case, many wrongs. Good or bad, I am who I am and proud of it. Now, I help others.

## International People

When I was working in the corporate world, I had the opportunity to travel the globe. It was interesting to see the differences in languages, religions, traditions, cultures, manners, upbringing, and attitudes. Business conducted in Japan was different as it was in Germany or Australia, BUT the one common denominator was people. No matter what the location or differences, we were all people with a mind, heart, and soul. Seeing and understanding this made my job so much easier.

## Old Times

I remember when I was a kid (yes, I was one once) the local meat market was only a few doors down. The drug store around the corner had a soda fountain and a magazine rack with comic books. A laundry/dry cleaner was next door to the meat market. The gas station at the corner was a Texaco. Yes, the owner had men in uniform checking the water, oil, tire air, washing windows, and filling the tank all at the same time. A duplex of businesses were sandwiched between the laundry and gas station. It had a barbershop on one side and a beauty salon on the other. The bus stop was at the end of the block and walking was not exercise, but a means of transportation.

We played tag, kick-the-can, dodge ball, and street baseball until it was dark. TV's were only watched during family time to shows like "Ed Sullivan Show," "Lawrence Welk," "Walt Disney," and "I Love Lucy." There were only three channels. The name for the local shopping mall was downtown, and it was open air.

Old time living was not only fun, but we also used our imaginations. Too bad things have gotten so simple now days.

## Parental Love

I was fortunate enough to have a well-rounded childhood. My father's parents immigrated from Italy, and my mother's parents from Sweden. This could explain a lot of my characteristics and demeanor. With that said, my sister and I were taught both cultures and traditions. My father worked his tail off sometimes working two jobs to provide for us, and my mother was a stay at home mom until we were in school. Then she worked part time for many years.

Looking back, it was the love that we had and shown everyday that we kept closest and maintain to this day. Yes, we got our butts whopped for doing wrong, not minding, or talking back, BUT we were hugged and kissed at every turn of our day (whether we wanted it or not).

Now with both of them gone, I would take a butt whoppin' or a hug and kiss in a heartbeat. I feel them with me all the time. I hope I was able to instill some of this love in our children, and I pray that you do too. That is what makes the difference, LOVE.

## Growing Up

My childhood was as normal as anyone else (I think). My sister and I received the same amount of love and attention. She strived for the honor roll, extra-curricular activities, and class offices. I strived for a "C," played music, listened to jazz, and being a kid. In any case, my parents were supportive of our decisions.

They supported and helped us to pursue our aspirations. In the end, my sister and her husband own a successful semi-monthly newspaper in a resort town in Wisconsin. I was a product of a global corporation with 32 years employment. They also gave us the latitude to make our own choices.

My father said to me while I was caring for him just before his death, "Mother and I wanted both of you to make your own decisions. If you screwed up, we supported your decision. We were always here to listen, but your decision is what made you who you are. Anyway, our pride and love for you two will always be the same." I want to be able to say the same thing to my kids.

## Dining Out

Outside of family gatherings, we went out to dinner occasionally for birthdays, anniversaries, and graduations. Our family did not have expendable money to spurge on things, but my parents made the most of what they had. We kids never knew our financial status because it was not important.

The restaurant choices were slim, but we either went to Maria's Italian Restaurant (of course) in the Italian section of town or to Bishop's Cafeteria downtown. Being as we went out so seldom, we could choose anything from the menu we wanted.

We quickly learned the art of "manners-in-public." We found out that dinner came to an extreme halt if we misbehaved and "doggie bags" came out to take things home. We also learned to follow instructions because it would be a long time before we did it again.

## Simple Life

Both my parents grew up in the Depression Era, so our financial status was never discussed in front of us kids. We did realize that a few of our relatives were a little better off. My sister and I received "hand-me-downs" from our cousins. Mom sewed some things for my sister. Anything new was given to us as gifts for birthdays and Christmas.

The older I got the more I realized that very little clothing that I had was new, but I also realized that our lives were not compromised because of it. We went to school with children of doctors, lawyers, politicians, etc. and that meant nothing to us.

I was the son of a box maker in a factory and proud of it. My mother was a school cafeteria cashier, and she was great at it. We didn't realize what social or financial status was. Isn't it amazing how things have changed? I think it all depends on which direction your nose is pointing.

## Normal Living

I think back when we made our own happiness and fun. We didn't depend on smart phones, computers, X-Box®, Play Station®, MP3 players, GPS, cable TV, wireless phones, and all else. We depended on our imagination to create games, mysteries stories, and hiding places.

Our friends were within a one-block radius of our house. We didn't lock our doors and windows. We wore our shoes out before we threw them away, and, in some cases, we had them repaired because we really liked them or couldn't afford new ones. We never bought a new car. We always bought used because the "bugs had been worked out" and we kept the car until it was finished. We used a push lawn mower, which was why we didn't let the grass grow too long. Was it a simple life?

It was simple from a technology aspect, but we had our problems. We had to use our imaginations, our physical strength, our families, our friends, and ourselves for everything. I believe it is how you look at simplicity and process it.

## Drivers' Ed

When we were learning to drive in high school, there were no instructions to drive and talk on the phone at the same time. For me, Drivers Ed was one of the classes that I feared. My instructor was the girls' PE teacher. I had heard nothing but horror stories about her. Needless to say, my attention was totally on what I was doing. It was drilled into my head to pay attention to everything. Of course, back then cars were not as easy to handle as they are today. Distractions are always going to be there. It is up to YOU to keep them to a minimum. Remember, the most precious cargo you have in the car is YOU. How many others are counting on you to make it to your destination?

## Patience

One thing that seems to be missing in this world is PATIENCE. It is almost as if everyone is in a hurry to get somewhere, buy something, finish something, and leave somewhere or even just live life. I hear horns honking, voices yelling, a fist shaking or a finger flashing at someone, or just mean stares.

It never fails if I am on the road; someone cuts in front of me only to stop at the next traffic light. They got upset for what? Only to say they are ahead of me. Come on people, take a DEEP breath in through the nose, and out through the mouth. Relax, enjoy life, and try taking one thing at a time. WE will live longer, smile a lot more, and love better.

## Mondays

It is amazing how many people look at Mondays is disgust or dread. We all make jokes about it, laugh at it, mumble and grumble our way through it, complain to everyone else about it, some grin at it, have fun with it, get in other peoples' face about it, and, yes, some even enjoy it. No matter what your theory is, there is nothing you can do to stop it. IT'S GOING TO HAPPEN! Therefore, I suggest, we make the most of it and live it like there is no tomorrow.

## Food

I grew up with an Italian father and Swedish mother. I acquired the Italian boisterous expressions of emotion, but the ability to set anger aside and reason the moment. I think my love abilities were a merger of the two.

The one thing that I have to thank both my grandparents for is FOOD. If things are a little rocky, "let's have some dinner, and we can talk about it," works every time! When I was in college (centuries ago), it was "Parents Weekend." I had some bad news, grade wise. When they came down to WIU for their visit and after dropping the bomb, they EXPRESSED their discontent, but ended it with, "Let's have some dinner, and we can talk about what we need to do."

Think about it, most of the world's problems have been resolved around food. I have declared that FOOD is the international ambassador to the world. EAT TOGETHER, RESOLVE PROBLEMS, BRING PEACE AND PROSPERITY TO THE WORLD (AND YOU), BE SATISFIED AND HAPPY!

## Beautiful Day

We were riding the East Bay Bike Path one day. Being such a beautiful day, we met many people also enjoying it along the way. Saying hello almost became a redundant, but still appropriate. The sun was bright; the breeze was blowing, creating a gorgeous day. These are the days that I cherish and am thankful for the most. I am with the love of my life, enjoying everything the world has to offer, being around "friends," and getting exercise to boot. There is nothing better than that. Another day to give thanks for the blessings I have.

## Like

No matter how hard you try to have people like you, there are always going to be those who just can't seem to grasp of the concept of "Like." Of course, you cannot force, buy, or threaten people to like you, and I know some who have tried. "Like" is just one of those things that you do or you don't based on your personal standards, preferences, or feelings. I know there are people who don't like me, but that is all right because they have their reasons whatever they may be. The point I am trying to make is that you are who you are, and people will either like you for who you are or not. Accept that point and you will live longer and happier. This is another reason I could never be a politician. They have to try so hard to have people like them just for a job. What a waste!

## Disappointments

We all have disappointments throughout our lives. There are things we count on that don't materialize, or things we thought we had, and it turned out that it wasn't there. I can go on about disappointments concerning events, relationships, job opportunities, winnings, and so on. Well, it is a sign of a mature person who can look these in the eye and make the most of what is left. The disappointment is only a step in character building, a strengthening exercise, or maybe just a plain ole kick in the ass. In any case, pick yourself up, dust yourself off, put your head down, and proceed to plow that path back to the road of success. Obstacles are only opportunities, not roadblocks (that's a quote from someone, but not sure who). Trust me, I know.

## Want To . . .

When I was growing up there was a cheer that we chanted at our high school games, "Ya gotta want it to get it" of course, the meaning was to win the game. We did our share of winning in those years at Rockford West High School, but it took me a long time to relate that saying to life in general. If you have the "WANT TO" burning inside, it is achievable. Sometimes you have to reach deep inside to know if there is a "WANT TO," but if it is there, IT is yours. This can be applied to anything jobs, money, relationships, hopes, dreams, or just life in general. So, my friends, do you have the "WANT TO" to get it? Then go for it.

## Rainy Saturdays

Rainy Saturdays are a great time to do some catching up, work on your hobbies, read a good book, or daydream about a sunny beach somewhere. ARE YOU FRICKING KIDDING ME? If you have kids, you are running to sporting practices, going to the mall, doing laundry, cleaning house, yelling at the kids to keep quiet, or, on a positive note, snuggling with your sweetie. In any case, it is still a day to rejoice and enjoy it as much as possible. Have a good one my friends.

## Wake-up Call

When I get up in the morning, I love to think about the wonderful blessings I have, the great opportunities I had, all the people I met or associated with, and all the loved ones in my life. Once my feet hit the floor, I have a smile on my face, a song in my heart, and excitement to face the day. I figured if I start the day with a positive feeling within, the rest of the day would follow suit. Even if there are bumps along the way, they are only small blips on the radar screen as opposed to the alternative where they seem like mammoth mountains. Been there, done that. It only shortens your life. Keep smiling.

## Sunday Morning

Childhood memories are always fun to remember. On Sunday mornings, my parents, my sister, and I religiously went to mass. It was during that time when you had nothing to eat since the night before in order to receive Communion.

When mass was over, us kids were no happy campers. We would go from church directly to "Lebunski Bakery." The aroma of warm bread, fresh from the oven, traveled at least three blocks away. Dad would be the one to make our purchase. My sister and I would sit with excitement wondering what he would buy. My mother, God bless her, put up with us alone in the car.

Finally, he appeared with two loaves of fresh bread and peanut rolls for us to have on the way home. We were in heaven. Isn't it amazing that fresh bread and peanut rolls were greater than Christmas at that point in time? We didn't have much, but we enjoyed what we did have.

## Self-Reality Moment

We have all done something stupid in our lives that embarrassed us with people around, but NO ONE knew. You know, you even blush at the thought of it, and people around you think, "What is going on?" This embarrassing moment makes you realize that you can be that stupid. If you can look yourself in the mirror and honestly say you have never had one of those, you really have not lived or experienced life. I call this a "Self-Reality Moment" (SRM). It tells you that you can be stupid, you are not perfect, and you are human like everyone else. It only means you love yourself.

## August 23rd

This is a "Bovi Holiday." When my kids were little, we would plan to do things but not put a date to it because we knew there was always the possibility that something could happen to prevent this becoming reality, either environmental or circumstantial. Well, my oldest son was persistent, tenacious, and kept asking, "When! When! When!" Our answer was always, "Soon" or "Sometime," as not to get their hopes up and face disappointment.

He haughtily came up with, "When, August 23rd?" out of nowhere. Well, that date had stuck, and to this day, we celebrate it as a major Bovi holiday. It has been with us for over 30 years and counting. It is just a little something that is our tradition. So Happy August 23rd to you and everyone, from all of the Bovi family.

## Getting Old

I keep thinking about "growing up" or should I say "getting older" or maybe "maturing" or how about "putting away the toys" or the good one "becoming of age" or the one that really gets me "reaching the second childhood". If you put it all together, how in the hell can you grow up just because we are getting older. If we were to be mature, would putting our toys away prove we are becoming of age, or are we reaching our second childhood? In any case, the federal, state, and local governments can categorize us. The corporations discriminate against us. The scams sap us of our money. HOWEVER, we can still get our discounts with AARP or AAA and spend our SS payment after the IRS takes what they need. We can budget for our balance after the CMS figures what, if anything, they will cover. I have always said there is no way I am getting old or allowing myself to think about it. I will just LMAO at the BS that scatters itself round. Are you joining me for a HELL OF A GREAT DAY? Well, it is going to be a memorable one because I have CRS and don't care.

## Focus

Integrity, honesty, workmanship, ethics, quality, pride, teamwork, empowerment, spirit, etc. are all the hot words I had collected while working in the corporate world. Someone had decided that these words would change the company's direction if everyone inside felt it too. Well, let me tell you something. You can use all the words and phrases they create. You can do all the exercises or programs they present. You can spend a ton of money on training or educating your employees you want. In the end, if it doesn't have HEART, PASSION, CARING, and most of all LOVE means nothing and will go nowhere. Gee, that fits into life in general and government too.

## Daily Song

"It's a wonderful day in the neighborhood. Won't you be my neighbor?" This was the opening song to Mr. Rogers. It drove me nuts when he sang it, the kids watched it and loved it, but it hits home now. I've given you something to sing in your head for the day. ENJOY!

## Do Your Best

The human race never ceases to amaze me. Being as I am included in this category of existence, I never cease to amaze myself either. To some, this may sound a little sarcastic, to others, it may sound egotistical, and another group might find that it hits home. When we were in school, they told us to do the best we can in whatever we do. Well, if we had followed that advice to the letter, we would have amazed ourselves. That is not being sarcastic or egotistical. It is just opening our eyes to the fact that if we give it everything we can amaze not only millions of others, but most importantly, ourselves. I sometime amaze myself for coming up with topics for this column every day. The foundation for everything is, love what we do and get the biggest joy from doing it. The greatest part is it's free.

## Stress

Stress is something that is inside of all of us. If someone tells me they are stress free, I would have to say "Bulls**t". There is not a person in the world that has not experienced stress. Mondays used to be one of my most stressful times, knowing I had to go to the office, take a trip, run to the airport, prepare for a meeting, turn in reports, answer any problems, or just plain old facing the traffic. I get a stomach ache just thinking about it.

I had a boss who always said, "I don't get stress, I give it," and he was half-right in that he definitely gave it. I determined it was all in how I handled the stress, putting things into perspective, and the help of friends, family, and God that pulled me through all of that. Everyone carries his or her stress differently, but one thing to keep in mind, YOU ARE NOT ALONE.

## Fear

Fear is an amazing feeling that helps us put things into perspective. There have been a few times in my life that straightened my hair (which is not a big feat, it is straight anyway). One of my most memorable times was when I went to China to review manufacturing facilities. I spent a week in Hong Kong with our sales manager before he sent me to Shanghai to meet with my host.

China, at this time, was not as free as it is today. My flight arrived around midnight. I was expecting my host to meet me at the airport, but two men in black suits greeted me with my name on a sign. Neither one spoke English. They bowed, took my luggage, and directed me to a black Mercedes limo. We drove two and a half hours inland China, passing two armed checkpoints and no streetlights so I couldn't see a thing. This was one time I placed my total faith in humanity and, yes, had a tremendous amount of fear.

During that week, I learned what REAL Chinese food was, invited to dinner for their home cooking, developed a friendship with people in a completely different culture, and grew an understanding of my fear. My hosts went out of their way to set me at ease.

I discovered that no matter where you are, people are the same. There may be physical, cultural, traditional, political, historical, or religious differences, but down deep, we are all the same. Fear is only something that we need to overcome within ourselves.

## Deception

I never took "The Art of Deception" course in college nor took a seminar or received personal instruction on how to deceive people with whom I worked. I was a "fat," dumb, and happy manager in my early years. I was confronted with a compromise, which I needed to give a lot of thought.

I once had an annual review that commented on me for not being able to hold confidential topics. The example given was when management informed me three days before our offices closed for good, and the people I worked with for almost 20 plus years ask me what is going on, I could not lie to them to say I didn't know.

This was one reason for ending my corporate career. How you look at your business ethics is one thing. If you need to compromise yourself for the job, then I can guarantee you will end up on the losing end. Remember, you have a conscience longer than you will have your job. Lying will catch up with you under any circumstances.

## Wednesday Fun

Well, my friends, we made it to the middle of the week, so at noon, yell at the top of your voice, "I am the greatest, the most wonderful person in the world. I am lovable, kind, friendly, and like everyone. If you have a problem with it that is too bad!", then just walk away. Enjoy a wonderful day.

## Hard Work

My parents were survivors of the Great Depression, and this meant that hard work was a part of our culture. I worked landscaping when I was 15. My sister sold shoes when she was 16. We learned that money is something you work for and not handed to you just because . . . We earned our allowance by doing chores starting from the time we were able to accomplish tasks.

Our mother made the majority of our school clothes. Our father would work two jobs in order to keep us in Catholic schools. We were not a fashionable family, but we had the proper attire for the occasion. We always had part time jobs during the school year and full time in the summer.

I see too much money handed to kids today for doing nothing. Sometimes it is a "pacifier" to keep them quiet. Even during these tough times, I see things given to kids with nothing done to earn it. We need to instill the value of money with our children, and they should realize the need to work for what they have. It really starts with US.

## Qualities

Facts, direction, trust, and truth are four words that set the tone for the future. We heavily rely on these words in our lives, relationships, business, or career. We look to our spouses, partners, colleagues, friends, bosses, owners, or our children to follow those four words to allow us to have faith. Do you have a relationship with someone who unquestionably gives you all four words comfortably? If not, they are the wrong person in your life. If so, this is someone who "deserves" to be considered a major part of your life. This is relative to anything, including elections. It is my four-point word check. If you waiver on any one of them, be careful.

## First Day of School

There are books of quotes and inspirational sayings. There are libraries and careers built on how we should live our lives and how we can be happy. There are websites and instructional videos on satisfying our need for all the things we are lacking in our lives. There are real live people available to help us with anything.

There is nothing to help fill that hollow void deep inside us when we watch our children leave for school for the first time. My daughter reminded me of this. She said that yesterday was the last day of daycare for our granddaughter. Even though I am a thousand miles away, that emptiness of them getting older hit me. BUT then again, the warmth of the thought that they are growing up seems to help fill it in.

## Grandparenting

Grandchildren give you the greatest feelings in the world. The only thing I can say to the parents who have not joined us in the "Grand-ranks", enjoy your children while they are growing up, teach them the best way you can, watch them as they develop into adults, pride yourself at their accomplishments, hug them as often as possible and as long as they will let you, and when it is time for them to expand their physical and emotional presence, be as excited as possible.

It is then that you are about ready to join the elitist crowd of grandparenthood. Believe me when I say, the sound of them seeing you and screaming your name with their arms outstretched running a collision course for you, receiving a hug so intense it takes your breath away, a kiss planted with precision accuracy, and them telling you how much they love you. There is no better moment than that. I love being a grandparent. I just wish I could be around all my grandchildren at one time. That would be better than winning the lottery.

## Labor Day, 2012

The city I grew up in had the normal parades, Memorial Day and Fourth of July, but they also had one for Labor Day. This was the first event of the year for the high school and junior high school bands. The trade unions would build floats to display their banners, and some of them would throw candy to the kids along the parade route. The one thing I definitely remember is there were no souvenir hawkers selling trinkets or snack or beverage stands selling their wares. Our sole purpose for being there was to watch the parade and enjoy the pageantry of the holiday. We kids would be so excited just to see everything that nothing else mattered, only the parade.

## 10 Secrets for a Good Marriage

Once, I asked my parents what their secret was for staying married for so long, 60 + years. Here is the list of things they believed in:

1. Never go to bed mad.
2. No matter how angry you are, there is ABSOLUTELY NO need for physical contact.
3. If you want to make a comment, which might hurt the other's feelings, don't say it.
4. If you did something wrong, don't try to hide it.
5. Revenge is not a solution to anything.
6. Never keep count.
7. Go for long walks and hold hands.
8. Listen to everything before making a comment.
9. Be honest with your feelings.

10. Tell one another you love them because you never know when it is your last.

To this day, I can hear our little talk over the kitchen table. I wish they were still here, so we could do it again.

## Talent

Talent is a big word. We all have it, but some will never know what theirs is. Others will look at it and not recognize it even if it slapped them in the face. Some realize it, but don't pursue it because someone had quoted the odds on succeeding. Then there are those who realize their talent, fine tune it, refine the presentation, and look for that break to put it out there for everyone to admire. It takes a leap of faith.

Most of us are afraid of failure and be ridiculed for thinking we could make it. Then some of us do not know what our talent is and continually change direction. In any case, one purpose in life is finding our talent, so start looking inside to find your greatness. It is never too late.

## Reassurance

Everyone growing up goes through a period when we feel a little insecure and need assurance to give us some stability. When we receive that stability, we feel stronger and ready to attack whatever we are facing. Who or what gives us that stability. For some, it will come from our parents, spouses, children, peers, bosses, friends, or us. Some will look for that reassurance from alcohol or drugs. No matter what the source, the main focus is on satisfying our need for a good old fashion pat on the back, the "atta" boy, good job, thanks honey, love you dad or mom, etc. To make us turn to alcohol or drugs, there is no one there to gives us our assurance fix including us. If you even have a feeling, that someone is reaching out for something, GIVE IT TO THEM. It may be saving them further pain.

## Parental Admiration

My father was a man who I admire and love. Looking back at my childhood, he was a disciplinarian and a loving person. I compared him with other fathers of my friends, and admired him for being able to keep us on a straight line, but be able to hug the living daylights out of us when it was time. I had my share of red buns for doing wrong, but I also had crushed ribs from his embraces. I had friends who were fearful of their fathers, mothers, brothers, sisters, or even "boyfriends" or "girlfriends." The only time I feared my father was when I knew I deserved it. Lung cancer took him from us while ago, but I talk to him every day and miss him and mom dearly. I REALLY tried my best to be like him. My only advice to fathers: when it is time to be the hard guy, do it within reason, but when it is time to recognize your children, do it with as much gusto as you can. THIS is what they will remember most.

## International Travel

During my corporate years, I traveled extensively, meaning I was not always home on weekends and most of those times not always in the USA. Fortunately, I had fantastic hosts who took time from their personal schedules to adopt me. This was a greater experience than if I was to go out on my own.

In Germany, I was able to see many things including the Black Forest and white asparagus fields. In England, I visited museums that are unknown to visitors and castles only read about in books. In South Africa, I saw Ostrich farms, the University of SA (which is a sight in itself), and diamond mines. In Australia, I visited "The Rocks," toured the bay and took a spin around the outback. In China, I saw what they consider a "farm" and learned their customs and traditions. In Japan, I was introduced to real Sushi, learned their meaning of honor, and made friends I will never forget. In Korea, I saw countrysides that were like nothing I had ever seen.

No matter where I went, I will remember always the friendships, local cuisine, home cooking, meeting the spouses, kids and pets, and getting acquainted with colleagues who I only see once year. This heartwarming experience will be with me to my grave. God bless them all.

## Family Day

Sundays were set aside for family. We always started out with Mass, bakery for hot bread, and home for breakfast. If we were hosting the dinner meal, it was time to put the dining room table together, pick things up and straighten the living room. All the while, mom was making the pasta, simmering the "gravy" (sauce or sugo), and final touches on the main course. If we were going to one of our relative's house, it was a little more relaxing, but still needed to make a dessert, salad, veggie, or "stuff." In all cases, we were around family almost every Sunday.

If we couldn't make it, we needed an acceptable reason like being either dead or close to death or in prison. Death was excusable, but prison was close to excommunication even though you could not make it for obvious reasons, but it was inexcusable. The family's advice to all was:

- Never die on a Saturday or Sunday (or they will be pissed)
- Don't screw up and wind up in prison (or they will be REALLY pissed)
- Enjoy the living hell out of your family no matter how big or small
- Always, always, always, love and hug them for who they are

Family is one reason you know how to love. Cherish every minute with them even if it is by phone, webcam, email, Facebook, Twitter, carrier pigeon, smoke signals, or actually in person.

## Good Morning

The alarm sounds; you feel a slight twinge of wanting to throw the damn thing through the wall; the head is a little foggy; the eyes can't focus; the legs feel like lead weights; every joint in the body aches; the bathroom beckons out of necessity; and you put a smile on your face anyway. You are granted another day to experience all you can; make friends; love others; learn something new; see beauty; hold hands; be kind to someone; make amends with an enemy; have fun; and just live today as if tomorrow is not going to happen.

## 911, 2012

Shock, fear, remorse, the anger are four emotions that can completely engulf a person to the point of being catatonic. That is what reigns over me every September 11th. I relive that morning, afternoon, and night every year. I remember the fear that ran through me because of the attack on our great country, the remorse for the thousands of lives lost that day and the many days to come after, the anger at those who caused our world to be turned upside down. Even after all these years, I still mentally relive the moments that redefined who we are not only as Americans, but also as human beings.

Give thanks to all those who are making our country and world safer, and give special thanks to our Supreme Being for keeping an eye on us and giving us strength.

## Politicians

I have respect for candidates who can tell me what THEY stand for, not their party, friends, neighbors, or the general population. I also would like to hear what THEIR plans are without telling me everything that is wrong now. WE know what is wrong. I just want to know HOW they will make it better. I would like to hear that they respect their opponent for what they had done because they feel they did the best they could without trashing their name. I respect those who run for office having their main purpose being to serve the people. I also have respect for candidates who say, I made mistakes and will do better. I respect candidates who have nothing to hide, good or bad.

I am tired of mudslinging, name-calling, dirt digging, and anything that degrades the opposition. If you are running for office, no matter what position, and if you have to resort to telling me how bad the other person is doing without giving a SOUND statement on HOW you would make a difference in 10 words or less, YOU DO NOT HAVE MY SUPPORT. If anything else, I will vote for "None of the above" (to quote Monty Brewster from "Brewster's Millions").

I have said before, I hate politics. I will only voice my opinion if I get pissed off enough. I will never publicly promote a single candidate. That is my business and prerogative. Have a great day, my friends. We have so much for which to be thankful. So, ask yourself this question, "Can I go a day without saying something bad about someone?"

## Kindness

Kindness is something that is close to my heart. I went to the market today (shock), and witnessed something that touched me. When I was leaving the store and returning to my car, I saw an elderly woman trying to cross the cross walk but one car after another cut her off.

The carriage collector was leading a long string of carts. He purposely started across the crosswalk and stopped. This allowed the woman and a ton of other people to cross the walkway. I had the biggest smile on my face watching the drivers having a fit because they could not do a thing.

I walked back into the store and reported the wonderful job their employee did helping others at their store. I thought that if someone went inside to complain, this kind employee would have been in trouble. Make sure you do something nice for someone today.

## MOM

My mother was a person who affected everyone she met. Her sweet personality, soft spoken voice, beautiful, fair complexion, magnetic smile, and a heart large enough to engulf the whole world couldn't be passed up by anyone. I had girl friends who after we broke up remained friends with my mother.

She would throw a good old fashion Italian Fiesta for my friends once a year with homemade ravioli, "gravy" (sauce or sugo), meatballs, sausage, salad, round steak with egg, cream puffs (zeppolis) and cannolis. Everyone thought they had died and went to heaven. This was quite a spread for a little (and I do mean little) Swedish girl.

If anyone could solve a conflict, she could. She has been gone for a little while now. Her last years were a slide with Alzheimer's and a failing heart, but the one thing she never lost was her ability to put a smile on our faces and a song in our hearts even up to the last minutes.

I always feel her with me, guiding me with her soft voice. Sometimes when I do something questionable, I can almost feel her "head duster," calling me an Italian name with a Swedish accent. I love you Mom and miss you dearly, like everyone else who knew you.

## Our Kids

If you aren't involved with your kids' lives, find a way to begin. Never become their best friend. Always keep a level head. Punish when necessary. Teach them to love our Supreme Being and respect for you and others. Love them with all your heart. You will never regret it.

## Rockford, IL

Growing up in a "small" Midwestern town, there were things that I was not introduced to until I was older. Small back there is a lot different from in New England. The town was one hour and twenty minutes northwest of downtown Chicago, "The Loop," an hour from Wrigley Field, and 50 minutes from O'Hare Airport. This all depends on the time of day.

It was located in the middle of corn country, population of about 125,000 back then. Now the greater Rockford Area is around 250,000. Reno has the title as being "The Biggest Little Town in Nevada." Well, we jokingly called our town "The Littlest Big Town in Illinois."

It was a great place to grow up without the hubbub and major problems of the big city and not the closeness of a country town. I was born and raised there. With everything said and done, it gave me my roots, my foundation, and helped me define who I am. For this, I am thankful.

## Personalities

Through my pervious careers, I have met many types of personalities. They include the pleasant, annoying, abrasive, funny, inviting, alluring, serious, focused, innocent, determined, compassionate, loving, etc. A few have no personality at all. Whenever I run into one of these, I used to feel sorry for them until I realized they don't know any better.

I think personalities develop from a person's foundation, education, experience, parental guidance, or direction, outside pressures, etc. Some of us realize that we are who we are and hone in on our own, but some of us allow others to mold us into whom we are not. These ones seem to have no personality.

Allow your kids to experience wonderful things, share yourself with them at all times, encourage them to be who they are and not afraid to reach out.

## Attitude

Mondays are either a pain in the ass or pure ecstasy. In any case, you have to go through it whether you like it or not. I prefer to be ecstatic than in pain. How about you? Have a wonderful and joyful day making everyone smile.

## Business Life

Ask me if I miss getting up at 3 AM, getting dressed and finish packing, drive an hour to the airport, hop a flight at 6 AM to get to my destination by 10 AM, their time, to make a meeting at 11 AM, lunch with the customers, post lunch meeting and wrap up, hoping to get back to the airport in time to make the 3 PM flight back home to arrive in time to make tee time for my youngest son's high school golf match or my older son's cross country meet or my daughter's Pompom halftime performance. HELL NO! The only things I miss are my kid's activities. Those are the only things I would give anything to do over.

If you feel stressed by reading this, I have more stories that will put your heart in your throat. My only advice is to opt toward your kids. You don't grow old with fond memories of your job, but you will with memories of your children or grandchildren. They don't need to know how hard you worked to get there to be with them, but you will, and being there is all that counts.

Give your son, daughter, sister, brother, husband, wife, grandchild, or anyone who is the significant person in your life the biggest hug and kiss you can. You never know if it will be the last. Grab the moment while you can.

## The Parents

My father worked in a factory and was proud to assemble corrugated cartons for the whole plant to ship their products. My mother had a part time job at the local junior high cafeteria, until my father suggested that they buy a tavern. That was what we now call "a leap of faith." For them, it was a matter facing financial disaster or family suicide. If there were ever icons for conservatism, they would be it because they were products of the depression. I remember both of them spending hours at night discussing the decision they had to make. When they finally made it, they spend sleepless nights worrying about what the future will bring.

They experienced many eye opening things, family problems, a sluggish start, setting a business plan for the first time, and putting things together to make it work. Years down the road, they had an extremely successful business.

The main point I carry with me is that they didn't give up on each other, no matter how stressful it got. There were times I thought this is it, divorce court here we come. One of the reasons for their longevity in their marriage was to "talk until it is resolved." They practiced this for over 60+ years. God bless them both and keep them in your love. They are my heroes.

## A Legacy

My Wife, children, and grandchildren are my ultimate treasures that will never be taken away. They are the ones who will carry on my legacy whether they know it or not. Most of all I have to say my wife needs most of the credit for keeping me sane, putting up with me every day (God bless her), puts up with my BS, ignores me when I get out of hand, and still loves me no matter what. SHE is my driving force whether she knows it or not. I love you, sweetie.

My children and grandchildren are my pride and joy who will have something of Grandpa Tony to carry forward. I look at my life as if it were a book. Page after page there is something to pass along to them. Great memories, life experiences, loving thoughts, and funny stories, all being something about which THEY would want to write. I only have this one chance to make an impact. I will not be just another parent.

Think about what you are leaving behind. Is it something that will fade with time, something that you will want forgotten, or something that will be cherished forever?

## Technology

Communication when I was young didn't consist of iPad®, iPods®, iPhones®, Androids®, Blackberrys®, cell phones, GPS, Kindles®, internet (what the hell was that) connections, 3G or 4G connections, Bluetooth®, wireless, etc. The most technical advancements were a telephone with a private line and the ability of getting three channels on our television (with luck and a little help from aluminum foil on the "Rabbit Ears").

If I wanted to get in contact with my next-door neighbor, it usually entailed sticking my head out the window and yell. That worked great if they were home. Winkie Dink was our only interactive television activity with the plastic screen and special crayons (if you need and explanation, let me know). The news came from the studio only. There were no remote news people.

Life was simpler back then, but if we were to relive it today with what we know now, we would be frustrated as hell. Progress is wonderful as long as it doesn't take away what is important, i.e. Family, Friends, and Us. Try not to lose sight of this.

## My Youth

When I was a kid, I marched with the local Drum & Bugle Corps starting when I was 12 years old. The experience comprised of dedication, education, and hard work, but it was fantastic for me.

Wintertime was to concentrate on learning new music for the coming season. Springtime was centered on the field presentation and fine-tuning the whole show. Summertime was marching parades and performing at competitions. We worked our tails off to perfect a show to compete with other corps across the nation.

Educationally, I got to know kids from other parts the country; that was when I realized New Englanders didn't pronounce A's and R's, learned what "y'all" meant down South, and found out what true bus travel was. I learned to live with the same people day after day and to get along with everyone, forming a family bond, and most of all enjoying every minute of it we could.

I am still VERY close friends with these "kids" from my youth, some on Facebook. It was all a part of who I am today. I would do this over in a heartbeat.

Rhode Islanders can see what I am talking about every year at the Bristol annual competition as a part of its 4th of July Celebration. It makes me remember how much fun I had and appreciate what it taught me. I still get a lump in my throat every year as it brings back memories.

## My Youth, part 2

I started Drum Corps when I was 12 years old. I didn't know anything about music, play an instrument, or know how to march. They placed a horn in my hands, told me to place the mouthpiece to my lips, pinch them tightly together, and make a squeaking sound. When I did, I played a pure high "C" which was quite an accomplishment for a first timer. THAT was the start of new life for me.

I learned how to read music, play brass instruments and play drums, learned to march, work together with others, and getting along with others in age ranges up to 21. The older members treated us youngsters as equals. It taught me age was immaterial when it comes to working toward a common goal. This formed my love and appreciation for music, which I carry to this day.

Periodically, I run across a picture from these days. It brings a lump to my throat and sometimes a tear to my eye. It will always be near and dear to my heart.

## The Drug Store

My wife and I were watching Diners, Drive-ins, and Dives® on Food Network, and they featured a place that had a TRUE soda fountain. We started to reminisce about our childhood. I had Carson's Drug Store (not the real name) around the corner from our home, and she had a similar store in the Buttonwoods area of Warwick.

Carson's Drug Store was our dispensary for the neighborhood. Mr. Carson was the ultimate of pharmacists. He was the first stop before going to the doctor. For normal itches and scratches, he suggested witch hazel or other natural cures. Anything that didn't clear up in a day or two, he advised to see your doctor. Nine times out of ten, it was resolved before that dreaded trip to the doctor.

There were two main features for the kids. The magazine rack that was huge. We read all the comics when they first came out. Mr. Carson's rule was "we could read the comics until he saw a wrinkled cover or torn page." Then there was the soda fountain, which was complete with a "Soda Jerk." It had all the trimmings. They served things like, Green Rivers, vanilla or cherry Cokes, chocolate, root beer, or vanilla phosphates, banana splits, HOT fudge, raspberry, strawberry, blueberry sundaes, and malts or shakes. The candy counter was classic with the jars of penny candy like buttons, taffy, kisses, etc.

Growing up was the hardest thing to do especially when we had to pass it every day going to school. It was an empty feeling when he finally closed his doors and retired. There just doesn't seem to be anything like this anymore in the neighborhoods.

## Life After?

I was thinking the other day about what happens after we die. You may think how morbid or WTF, BUT how about a different scenario. Our accomplishments, here on earth, are our legacy for this world, which we hand off to our children and grandchildren. This is not the end of our eternal trek.

After a slight rest in "limbo" before our next "assignment," we advance to the next step in our existence, which is based on our last performance. If we are a person who showed love, kindness, giving, creativity, etc., we are awarded a life that is equal to what we learned in this life. If we were a person who was not kind, loving, giving, creative, etc., we digress to a position, which gives us a second chance to take a "Mulligan" on life.

We have no true memory of the past only periodic "glimpses" to help us understand why we are where we are (déjà vu). The one thing I have not determined is whether we come back to earth or to another planet. Let's face it, God created a universe that is never ending, so not having another place for us out there is doubtful.

The objective is to learn to follow the right path. If we pass this test, we become exempt from the next step and given the eternal life, we deserve. I know it sounds absurd, but then again, maybe not. Think about it. There is always time to make a change in our lives.

## High School Years

My high school experience was great, but not like the rest of my friends. Being as I was not heavily involved in sports, class government, or the "popular" crowd, I don't think there were too many who really knew me. One thing I did do was play the "Charge" tune on my bugle during football games, did some pranks on the administration (nothing illegal, that came in college), and joined glee club because my love for music.

I suppose I might have been considered one of the "geeks," but this didn't make a difference to me because I knew the opportunities and experiences I had that everyone else didn't. Learning music, discipline, communication, camaraderie, cooperation, bus travel, sharing everything with everyone, and just plain old hard work were all a part of my educational experience.

Book learning was important for advancement in school and my ability to go to college, but I will say it was not on the top of my list priorities. I was happy with a "C." Was I happy with my high school years? Hell yes! It was just a little different from everyone else.

## Life's Lessons

The Drum Corps (DC) activities, I write about from my childhood, were paid for by a low-to-middle income family. The experiences my sister and I had were only due to my parents' sacrifice and our own blood, sweat, and tears. The majority of our drum corps friends did the same thing with full time, part time, or odd jobs. Those who were able to afford this on their own were no different from the rest of us. Money was not a determining factor for anything.

What was important was attitude, working hard, wanting to win, and having the time of our lives, which we did with great gusto. None of us got in trouble or arrested. The Three Musketeers saying, "All for one and one for all" held true for us.

Being out of contact with the DC world, I am not certain how much of this is still evident or even pertinent in today's groups. No one blamed or pointed a finger at one another. There was no tolerance for bullying, or if an incident happened, the kids took care of the situation with no harm to anyone.

All said we were family of a hundred plus kids. Not anyone not fitting into our family, which was highly unusual, was welcome, but everyone had a chance. THAT was a BIG lesson learned not only then, but also now.

## Learned the Difference

On one trip with the Drum Corps in the early 60's, we were in the southern most town in Illinois. We were there for a parade and competition. Being as it was a 10-hour trip from the top of state to the bottom of the state and NO interstates and very few four-lane highways existed, we arrived a day early to rest up for the following day.

After morning rehearsal, a group of about ten went to lunch at a local restaurant. We were all hot, hungry, and thirsty. We went in and asked if we could move tables together for all of us to sit. Given approval, we rearranged the furniture and sat down.

The waitress came over and asked one of our members to leave. We asked why because he didn't do anything wrong. She explained to us that he was "colored," and they don't serve "colored" people in their place. Dead silence hung in the restaurant from shock for all of us. We had heard of this happening, but we never experienced it coming from northern Illinois.

All of us got up, moved all the furniture back to where it was, and left. The owner saw a lot of money walk out the door and came after us asking what was wrong. Our response to him was, if you cannot serve our friend, we couldn't be served either. We had many delivered meals for the next two days.

The experience gave us a new perspective on the world and its warped ways. From that point on, we were VERY aware of what discrimination was all about.

## Saturday Thought

Saturday is one of the most wonderful days of the week, well, along with Sunday, and ahh Friday, and of course Wednesday, but Thursday isn't so bad, oh hell Monday is good, shit, that being said Tuesday is alright too. I suppose any day when you wake up in the morning, heart beating, breathing in and out, and feeling pretty good can be considered wonderful days.

## The "H" Word

Have you ever looked at the definition of the word "HATE"? It includes words like despise, loath, extreme hostility, detest, etc. My grandson learned in daycare never to use the word "HATE." He corrected us adults when we made a statement using that word. He would so eloquently say, "Never use the word HATE. It is not nice." I was proud to hear this and even learned to dislike the word myself.

Yes, there are people who piss us off. There are things that we might not like to eat, the taste of, the sound of, the color of, the feel of or anything. Using the word "HATE" is pretty strong and harsh. I have to commend my grandson for making us think about that word whenever we use it when speaking about things in general.

When we direct it at a person, think about the people themselves. I would not like someone "HATING" me. I would care less if they disliked me, could not stand me, were disgusted with me, extremely upset with me, or even as simple as disowning me. To HATE me would be an all out insult.

Let's put a stop to hatred and vow to try and never say the word HATE again. If you run out of synonyms, let me know. I will send you a link for a great Thesaurus to help you out.

## Teenage Loves

There were times in high school that it was a little difficult balancing school and Drum Corps (DC). I mean social activities. Being so wrapped up into DC that I forgot about such events as homecoming, dances, proms, plays, etc. Some dates were impromptu partially because of my lack of planning.

I took a girl to Senior Prom who was engaged to a person in the Air Force stationed in Vietnam. She was in homeroom with me. I knew the circumstances and asked her to go with me. She asked her fiancé. I talked with him on the phone, got his approval, and the rest was history. We enjoyed the evening, and I even got a thank you from the boyfriend.

Homecoming was not a formal event like it is today. It was attended with date, stag or in a mixed group. I did have a girlfriend in my first year in college, but she lived in Casper, WY, again because of DC. In my sophomore year, there was a special someone a little closer to home, Chicago. That was the other DC relationship.

Knowing people from all over was inevitable, and, when we spent four months with these people, day in and day out, we developed feelings. I am still friends with many of them today. Of course, there were difficult times with breakups, upsetting moments, and normal love bumps and bruises, but the great times far outweighed the negative ones a thousand fold. It was a good lesson in love.

## The Snow Storm

I was waiting for an appointment to arrive the other day, and thought about the times I was on the road making sales calls. I tried hard to be a considerate sales person and did everything I could to get to the appointment at least 15 minutes ahead of the designated time, even if it meant waiting in the car.

Well, there were times when shit happened. Accidents, traffic problems, car problems, weather problems, etc. which always warranted a phone call with an apology, a request for delay and reschedule the meeting, and a sincere word of appreciation for their understanding. Cell phones were not in existence at this time. We needed to find a place, park the car, and make the call from a pay phone.

The most memorable missed meeting was in St. Paul, MN. I was there with my bosses, the VP of Sales, and the division President. The evening before the meeting, we were at the hotel going over the final details of the presentation the next day. We enjoyed a great meal, a nice glass of scotch, and called it a night.

The next morning I did my usual routine, wake up, turn on the TV, start the coffee (yea, even back then they had coffee makers in the room), and take care of "necessities." I walked back to see the weather guy stating that the "Golden Shovel" award went to St. Paul, MN with an unexpected snow fall of 14 inches in a six hour period of time. Without hesitation, I ran to the window, whipped open the curtains, and saw the award-winning layer of snow. Thank God, no one was in the parking lot, or they would have had a little more than snow to look at.

The lesson of this day was there are things we have NO control over, so make the most of what we have and use it to the best of our ability. It was an opportunity for my superiors and me to get to know each other a lot better. Sometimes shit happens for a reason. ( . . . for you business people, we gave the presentation one day later and awarded the contract.)

## Merging

Driving over to the West Bay in Rhode Island the other day and merging onto I-195 in East Providence, there were not that many cars on the westbound side. The one car in the lane I was merging into sped up and blocked me from getting on the Interstate. I sped up, he sped up, I slowed down, and he slowed down.

Merging is a phenomenon, which is misunderstood by many Rhode Island drivers. They either come to a complete stop at the bottom of the ramp, slow down to a crawl to ease into the lane, or the race like hell and see if anyone challenges the action of merging. The correct way is to increase speed on the ramp to equal that of the merge lane, and the cars in the merge lane are to allow you space to enter the highway. THAT is how to merge.

The objective here is NOT allowing anyone entering the highway ahead of his or her vehicle. You get crowded out, pushed off, honked at, given the "finger", mouthed obscenities, slammed fists on the steering wheel, slapped foreheads, raised fists, and pursued to the extent of being cut off. Peace and tranquility happen only outside of the car.

Has anyone realized all of this gives you high blood pressure, indigestion, shortens your life, maybe even provoke a heart attack or stroke, or even death ending not only your life but potentially others too. All of this for what, a two second delay to allow one car in front of you. God forbid! Take a little time, live longer, and save lives, mainly your own.

## Elderly Lady, New Friend

I mention quite often about putting smiles on peoples' faces. There was a woman, who lived across the street from us when we were 8 or 9 years old. I estimate her age being in her 70's, at the time. We never saw her smile. She owned the home and rented the second floor to a young couple with no kids. I do not think she had any children or relatives because no one visited her.

I asked Mom if she was a witch or a mean old person. Mom being mom, the sweetest person in the world, just said that she had no one, has never talked to anyone in the neighborhood, and calls the neighborhood meat market for her groceries to be delivered. The only time she left the house was to go to "church" on Sunday morning. We didn't have malls back then, so that was out of the question.

One Sunday, we went to Mass early because we had the family gathering for dinner that day. I decided to find out for sure if this woman was a witch, a nasty person, or just sad. My plan was to wait until she got home and run over to meet her. Yea, I was gutsy at that age.

When I saw her car coming down the street, I ran over to the house next to hers, waited for her to park, and get out of her car. I walked over shaking like a leaf, sweat on my forehead, hands shaking, and scared to death, but my determination was strong along with my curiosity.

As she got out of her car and ambled toward her house, I walked up to her, introduced myself, and held out my hand. For the first time in my life, I saw the start of a smile come to the corner of her mouth. She shook my hand and said, "It is nice to meet you, young man. I am Mrs. Grogan. I have seen you and the rest of the kids play in the street and wished I had children to keep me company." She thanked me for visiting with her and asked for us kids to stop by anytime to have lemonade or cookies.

From that point on, I never underestimated the power of a smile, the shock of a surprise handshake, or even a simple hello. The people, who do not respond, deserve to be miserable and those who even put just a curl on their lips, deserve a hug. We are here to love one another. It is up to us to do just that.

## Knowing Yourself

The first year of college was a challenge for me. I went to a brand new junior college, lived at home, paid for a car, had a part time job, and unclear as to what the hell I wanted to do when I grew up (here I am, 65 plus years old, and still asking myself that question). In the inaugural year of this school, daytime classes were at a Naval Reserve center in the South end of town, and the evening classes were at a high school in the North end of town.

The second semester was the ball buster. I had a 4 o'clock at the reserve center and a 6 o'clock at the high school. The travel time between locations was about 30-45 minutes depending on traffic. Dinner was eaten in transit, which consisted of a P&J sandwich, chips, and apple. I was only allowed a hot meal on Fridays, Saturdays, and Sundays.

I was an engineering major for 5 days, an education major for 2 weeks, a psychology major for 2 weeks, and non-committed for the rest of the year. I excelled at public speaking, creative writing, music, psychology, and mythology, so I pursued a career in business administration. That makes sense . . . how? I did well at that career for 35 plus years.

I learned more about myself in that one year than I did throughout my total education. It was something I would not have learned if I graduated with a Masters or PhD degree. I learned how to cope with personal difficulty, maintain a tight schedule, make car payments with minimum of income, hold down a part time job, dislike rush hour traffic, make new friends after high school and Drum Corps, deal with difficult people, discover things I can and cannot do, and unbelievable things about myself, which began the mold of who I am today.

Many people look back and say, "I wished I coulda, woulda, shoulda, or wanted ta". I never regretted anything I did. I took advantage of everything I could and lived life like there was no tomorrow. It taught me something that I later lost and have regained. Life, itself, is what you make it. If you feel, it is dealing you misery that is what you will have. If you open yourself up to everything, it has to offer, it will pay you back tenfold. No matter how dim or miserable things seem now, you need to have perseverance, tenacity, and faith in yourself. IT WILL HAPPEN.

## One Resolution to Bullying

I read an article concerning bullying and the effect it has on others. Growing up, I had my share of name-calling and hard times. One of my classmates and I were the shortest kids in our grade school. We were the center of attention. The answer for me was to be able to run faster and longer than anyone else; however, my fellow "Shorty" carried his determination a little further in his life. He was a strong student, had high logic abilities, and compassionate to others. He became an Illinois Supreme Court Judge. Think about that if you were a bully to him and needed to stand before him in court.

Here are a few suggestions I have used in the past:

1.   Find a shell that you can place around you and not let anything or anyone penetrate it. Focus on your mission which is YOU.
2.   If you feel you can do something (anything) that you love and do well, go for it. Look deep inside yourself. Look for that one thing that makes you happy. It can be anything like writing poetry, painting, drawing, singing, belly dancing, talking, teaching,

learning, playing a musical instrument, loving, negotiating, giving, organizing, etc. Every one of us is on this earth for a reason. It is up to us to find it and excel at it. We cannot let one bully or loud mouth stop us from succeeding.

3.  WHEN you find that one thing, do not let anything or anyone stand in your way to pursue your path to greatness. The only thing that will stop you is you. There will be tons of negativity in that path but be tenacious and strong. I gave up too many times, but I still pursue what I want to do and try to do it to the best of my ability.

4.  WHEN you have reached that point where you feel comfortable that you have found what you wanted to do, pass what you learned to others. This way you will encourage them to pursue their passion.

If you are reading this, you have learned what I wanted to do for a long time. The bullies can call me anything they want or treat me as horrible as they want, but I work at what I love to do every day. They might not be able to say that, so it sucks to be them.

## Memories

Many memories are created at times you least expect it. These are not gatherings like weddings, anniversaries, birthdays, baptisms, graduations, etc. These memories happen with all the normal activity of everyday life and are those spontaneous moments that will remain in your mind forever.

None of the memories I write about were ever caught in snapshots, Instagrams, JPEGS's, PDF's, DVRs, VHS, DVD, or so on. These events are engraved in my memory only. I can either let it rot in my storage unit or open it up for others to enjoy. I elect to share my life experiences with you. Some may be boring as hell to you, but it might be meaningful to someone else.

I post my life because I want you to know whom you or I wanted as a friend. I feel I have something to offer everyone. Take away from it what you want, leave what you don't need, and enjoy whatever turns you on. I can guarantee one thing will never change . . . me. Like me or dislike me, that is totally up to you, but I have things to share with all.

Hopefully, I can help someone start a new life when they feel it is hopeless or bring some happiness to those who feel there is nothing to smile about or just entertain you with a story. In any case, I am who I am. If you ask my best friend, my wife, she will tell you I am annoyingly positive in the morning and increasingly up for the rest of the day. I am constantly looking for the positive in everyone and all situations, and I am sweeter than maple syrup. Everything said I love people, my friends, my children, my grandchildren, MY WIFE, and everyone who will be with me to the end of . . . . This will be your call.

## Columbus Day, 2012

Happy Columbus Day! I have to say this day was never a holiday when I was a kid. Yes, it appeared on all the calendars but we still went to school. It was a day of reverence to the person and crew who found the wonderful country we live in. He was an Italian who was funded by the King and Queen of Spain to take the trip to prove the earth was not flat and discover whatever there is to find.

They discovered a land that provided everyone an opportunity to grow, to avoid religious oppression, to be a dumping ground for undesirables, to create rebels and fortune seekers, but most of all to begin a new life. Little did they know they found a gold mine. It turns out that the territory would help bring peace and support for millions around this "flat earth."

This land in its time has been through so many changes, adjustments, and fine-tuning, but it still survives through it all. Feel good about where we live. We have a better way of life than others have in the world trust me. It all started with a little Italian who just wanted money to prove someone wrong. Look where we are today. Thanks Chris. You did well.

## Birth of a Daughter

My daughter's birthday will always remind me of the day she was born. It was a chilly day. I had volunteered to help my brother-in-law for Lions Day looking for donations and in return, they would receive a roll of LifeSavers. When I finally arrived at the office, my wife had called to say that things were beginning to happen. Being not in the mindset of what this meant, I asked her what was happening. She stated, "Our baby!"

At that time, my heart went straight for the throat. I choked on the coffee, gasped for air, fell back in my chair, grabbed my lunch and briefcase, threw on my jacket, told my assistant I was leaving, and raced out of the door. I found out later that I never hung up the phone and coffee spilled over my desk. In any case, what was normally a 30-minute drive took maybe 15. Once home, my wife was understandably uncomfortable, but nothing regular for contractions. I sat at the kitchen table, opened my lunch, and proceeded to eat it. My wife asked me what I was doing, and my only comment was that I wasn't sure when I would be able to have lunch.

Well, things progressed and off we went to the hospital. While I got her checked in, she was brought to "The Floor." When I arrived to the room, things had progressed but not fast enough. Lamaze was not doing what it was supposed to do, probably because we were not thinking about that. We kept holding our breath and the nurse kept telling us to breath. Evidently, we were both turning weird shades of color. Our regular doctor was on vacation, which left us with a substitute that meant I would not be allowed in the delivery room. My wife was in tremendous pain, and I felt like the most horrible husband ever for causing this. The only positive aspect of this was progress with each visit from the nurse.

Finally, what seemed like years, it was TIME. I saw the fear in my wife's eyes as she was rolled away. I felt alone, helpless, scared, fearful, and yes excited. I prayed like never before. I stared out the window as the warm sun was shining in on me. I was trying to visualize what my wife was going through and tears were filling my eyes.

When the nurse came in to ask if Mr. Bovi was here, I turned to see a smile on her face, which sent all fears out the window. She said that everything was normal, mother is doing fine, and I was a father of a beautiful baby girl. She directed me to the end of the hall where mommy and little girl would be come out soon.

Shortly, my wife was being wheeled down the hall followed by an incubator. I grabbed her hand, kissed her, and smiled. Looking into the incubator, I looked closely at her; she opened her eyes, and looked directly at me. I just said, "Hi Heidi." It was almost as if she smiled at me. Here was the most beautiful little daughter in the world, only minutes old, and did not have a clue what to expect next, but none of that mattered. At that very minute, my heart grew to an astronomical proportion to my body, and it still is growing.

THAT MOMENT WILL BE WITH ME FOREVER.

## Respect

Everyone is different, thank God. Each of us not only looks different, but we all have different traits, styles, shapes, personalities, tastes, mannerism, sexual preferences, physical make up, and most of all faith. It can be a religious faith, non-religious faith, or personal faith. In any case, that molds us into who we are. Yes, some of us are Catholic, Jewish, Protestant, Hindu, Islam, Episcopalian, Lutheran, Buddhist, Agnostic, Atheist, etc. We all have brains to think and believe in what we want, how we want, when we want, and with whom we want.

We praise a higher power in our own image. If we use a tenth of our brain for what it was intended, it would tell us that we should RESPECT others for who they are. This individuality makes this world what it is. That RESPECT should be open to love, growth, kindness, beauty, creativity, acceptance, and abundance. With this change of mindset just think of the possibilities, we might have, PEACE. May we all find it and live it.

That is my Sunday morning SBS (Soap Box Sermon).

## The Old Neighborhood

When my parents were still living, my wife and I would go back "home" for visits. Outside of the fun of sitting around talking and reminiscing, we would always bring up the old neighborhood and what made it so special and memorable. Some of the things made us laugh; others gave us warm feelings, but mostly were the descriptions of houses, people, mannerisms, quirks, and, yes, just plain weird things.

Wanting to show my wife the place where I grew up, we took a drive to the "Hood." We drove slowly pointing out where people lived, the stores, gas station, schools, routes, and the special points of interest. The one thing that will always stay in my mind, it was nothing like I remembered. Landmarks were no longer there, houses were falling apart, lawns were no longer showpieces, and the warmth of home was missing.

For my wife, it was putting the stories into perspective, but, for me, it was a disappointment and the realization of never going back thinking it would be the same. It provided the determination to cherish the memories even more and enjoy them as if they still existed.

## Final Moments

My wife passed on to me a great saying, "One day your life is going to pass before your eyes, so make it worth watching." THAT is what life is all about. This is what I have been passing along to all of my friends. I think this is one reason why it took both my father and mother so long to pass on. They lived their lives to the fullest, and it took them that long to relive every minute of it. This probably didn't include the time it took to share it with the rest of the family who passed away before them.

If it means prolonging my final moment, I will warn my kids and my wife now. They had better plan on carryout for dinner, fire up the oven for breakfast, and possibly invite the neighbors in for leftovers. With all the travels, people I have met, and adventures experienced would be just the introduction and will not include the main plot or characters. In short, this is one show worth watching the rerun.

## Business Travel

I overheard someone talk about having to fill out an expense report for work after returning from foreign travel. They had to convert from the foreign to US currency. It made me snicker to myself. I remember filling out my expense report for a trip from hell. Starting out in Hong Kong, going to Taiwan, heading to Korea, jumping to Japan, layover in Shanghai, and finally heading to Australia for the final stop before returning home. This report was a masterpiece and worth keeping. For anything else, it was a reminder of what it represented, a three and a half week trip providing me with memories and pictures to last a lifetime. It was worth every single pain in the ass minute to finalize it. It also taught me to enjoy and experience everything you can no matter how miserable you feel at the time.

## My Business Career

Looking back at the classes in which I excelled at, I probably should not have taken the career path I did. Speech, Algebra, Geometry, Calculus, Statistics and Probabilities, Accounting, Psychology, Sociology, Creative Writing, Bowling, Swimming, Mythology, Drama, and Social Interaction were the ones that I excelled. The ones I didn't really do well were, General Business, Marketing, Advertising, Zoology, History, Political Science, and Art Appreciation. How and why I ended up in Marketing is beyond me?

With all those years behind me, I look back to say the job market was not the greatest. I took a job as an inspector at a screw factory until one opened as an expediter in an automotive parts company. The boss left for another company and hired me to be a manufacturing planner for a medical supply company where I worked for the next 33 years.

Overall, I cannot say my education was important to get me where I was; however, the passion for the products we made, and customers we served were what kept me there. The mechanics of the job were self-taught. I took the initial job just to make money, the second job was a step into business, and the third job was the door to a future, which took four years from start to finish. Patience was the factor.

## Imaginations

Are you helping instill imagination in your children? If you question yourself, ask your little one to tell you a story about anything he or she wants. You may have to start things, but they should be able to hold on to something of a story for a while.

My kids did this when they were young. Of course, these stories would become embellished when they started driving, dating, during grade time, doing homework, notification of parent meetings and notices, etc. They were not lacking in the imagination area at that age. I could write a book, "1001 Excuses."

It became a ritual to tell my kids stories at bedtime about two squirrels, Nutsy and Cutesy, whom they have now passed down to their children.

We also had finger puppets, "Ferdinand and Buford," who were the center of many stories. This was something I tried to do as often as possible.

As parents, we are the ones who cultivate that imagination, not the teachers. If we start, it will help grow and create their thoughts and stories. Spend a little time to get their juices rolling. Think about it, you or they might be able to write a story or two later in life.

## Sundays at the Bovi's

Sundays were the greatest days in our house for food, family, friendship, and love. Mom and Dad would make us wash our faces, clean our ears, comb our hair, put on our Sunday best, and off to mass we went.

We were members of St. Anthony's Church, which was out of the parish in which we lived, but Dad was an usher, so he had to be there. Mom would march us down the aisle while Dad took care of his responsibilities. I will say my actions were not always the best, but for the most part, I was tolerable.

Afterwards, it took forever to leave because of all the friends my parents had. I had my cheeks pinched continuously, so that may be the reason they were out of proportion to the rest of my face. When I smiled, I look liked I appeared to be squinting, but in actuality, my cheeks pushed my eyes closed.

The highlight after mass was picking up warm bread at the bakery, home for breakfast, and off to a relatives or friends house for dinner or just a visit. In all circumstances, we always left time to be at Mom's side of the family for at least a short period. In ALL cases, it always involved food.

When we finally got home, we were exhausted, Mom and Dad got lunches prepared, coffee ready to turn on in the morning, beds turned back, stories told, and my sister and I tucked in for the night. From that point on, I have no knowledge of any existence of life. Once, I asked Dad what he and Mom did after we went to bed. All he did was smile. It was a father's way of saying, "DON'T ASK."

Looking back, it was a fairly, normal childhood, but it will ALWAYS be special for me. Take the time to make your own memories for your kids. It will give them stories to tell their children. Those times give me material to write forever.

## Grade School

My parents sent us to the local Catholic grade school, St. Peter's School. Mom walked with my sister and me to school every day. We took that seven-block hike in rain, snow, heat, blowing wind, sub-zero weather, etc. She would also meet us after school to walk us home. When my sister was old, enough to "watch over me," she became the protector and Mom wished us farewell from our front door. My sister was three years older, so as we aged the less concern there was for the little brother. She only attended the school up to the seventh grade when she transferred to a public Junior High.

Here I was in fourth grade and lost my security blanket or protective shield. I grew up fairly quick that year. The older kids became aware that I was unprotected. That was when the taunting on my height became an issue. I found out that my sister was a bigger buffer than I thought.

Fortunately, I survived and things were fine for the rest of my time at St. Peter's, and I don't think I ever thanked her for being my guardian angel for those first three years, but she knows I appreciate all she did for me. Things were definitely different back then.

## Decision Time

At the beginning of the week, we have a choice. Do we want to look at the day in a positive manner? Do we want to think that this is one of the greatest days of the week? Do we want to believe we can do anything we wish this week? This is the BIGGEST opportunity we have to make a difference in our life and maybe the life of someone who needs it. Make the difference.

**Our Garden**

Dad had a garden in the backyard. He grew all our summer vegetables and Mom would do all the canning for the winter. He grew, of course, tomatoes, but also beans, lettuce, rhubarb, potatoes, beets, parsnips, and carrots. Out of all the stuff they grew, the things I could not stand were beets and parsnips.

In the back of the garden, Dad had a very well protected grape arbor. Mom made all our grape jelly. There was a passageway behind our garage from the neighbor's yard to the grape arbor. The neighbor boys tried to steal the grapes, but Dad had rigged up an alarm system with tin cans and string. He terrorized the neighbor boys with his bounding voice and snapping a leather belt that made the noise of a shotgun.

Everyone knew how fun loving Dad was but very few grapes disappeared. None of these precious gems went for wine. That was left to the experts in "Little Italy" (South part of town) when Dad received a bottle or two during Christmas time.

Whatever came out of our garden supplied our needs for the winter. Mom's sugo came from homegrown tomatoes, home dried herbs and spices, onions, and garlic. Were we "organic"? What the hell was "organic"? It came from the garden. It was springtime when you could smell dirt, fresh cow manure, and wet straw. If that is organic, so be it.

**MorFar (Mother's Father)**

My Swedish Grandfather, MorFar, was quite a fisherman and hunter. He was the father of four girls, so he needed to provide for them as much as possible during the toughest time in the depression. Mom told me what he did to put food on the table. Fish, crayfish, rabbit, squirrel, duck, goose, and deer were always on their menu.

I remember going fishing with him at a piece of property he owned on the river. We left on a Saturday morning in his old Dodge which never made it over 40 mph on the highway. It took us at least an hour to get there, which in today's traffic would be 20 minutes tops. He was the most patient man ever created. He taught me how to hook a line, bait the hook, cast off, and, most importantly, WAIT AND BE QUIET. In the few hours we were there, he caught five catfish to my one perch. In his Swedish accent, he made me feel like that little perch was a marlin out of fresh water.

When we got home, we had the perch for dinner. More than likely, dinner included a few of his fish too, but that made no difference to him. It was my fish providing our meal. He taught me more in those few hours together than I could have learned in a lifetime. He was one man who had my heart from that day on. That's what grandpas are for.

## Wednesdays

Wednesday is one day of the week that reminds us how much of a positive outlook we have on life. The two questions we ask ourselves is how much shit can we pack into the next two days to really accomplish something, or, on the other hand, can we blow off the next two days and get that shit done next week? I prefer to pack it in. That leaves next week open for something new.

## MorMor (Mother's Mother)

My Swedish Grandmother, MorMor, needs to be commended for so many things that I just don't know where to start. Outside of her Swedish accent and petite stature, she was soft spoken, one of the most accomplished Swedish knitters, crotchetier, and cooks in the world.

Like the gospel about turning fishes and loaves of bread into a meal for thousands, she could turn a refrigerator of crap in to a gourmet meal in minutes. I have no idea what or how she did it, but when everyone would show up on a Sunday afternoon, she did her magic. She would present an exquisite meal. She was also the one who taught my mother to do the same thing. Swedish cooking was not known for their use of spices, but they lived in the middle of "Little Italy," so she learned how to use oregano, sage, rosemary, thyme, basil, etc. and religiously.

The Italians in the area adopted them. MorFar would get a bottle of homemade wine every Christmas from the men, and MorMor went to the cookie baking gatherings. Seeing native Swedes and Italians living amongst one another and accepting each other into their homes was heartwarming. Why can't we do that today? Too busy?

## Celebration

Today is a day of celebration. We need to jump up and down and yell our living heads off. WHY, you may ask? Well, we have this day to make the most out of it, have loads of fun, and spread all the love we can. We have to take every advantage we can and put a smile on our faces for everyone to see.

## Misery Stands Alone

There is an old saying that I know you have heard before, "Misery enjoys company." I have a real problem with this statement. Of course, misery enjoys company because no one wants to face emotional crap alone. If anything else, they go out of their way to convince others to join them. It even comes down to manufacturing misery. Yes, there are a very few people who are willing to join them.

Why would anyone volunteer to be miserable? Hello!!! Most of us fight like hell trying NOT to be miserable. There are therapists, medications, coaches, teachers, clergy, inspirational people, counselors, or even nuts like me to help rid anyone with misery. All it takes is reaching out and requesting help. That is THE biggest step for anyone to make in an attempt to achieve happiness. My favorite saying is, "Smiling is contagious. Try it. You might like it."

## Priorities

This election is nearing to a close. The last push is in process. ALL candidates are battling for the last vote. Charges are flinging around like pompoms. Falsehoods created to encourage your decision. Truths are being stretch farther than small-sized pantyhose on a large person (woman or man pending their preference). Accusations thrown around like M&M's. Polls are calculated based on God knows what. Yet the main thing is life goes on. No matter what the outcome of this election is life will not stop on its outcome. All media reports are to make us feel that everything hinges on this one day. Yes, we need to take part in this "EVENT" because it is our RIGHT. If we do not exercise our RIGHT, we have no basis to bitch about the outcome.

Look at all the other close races in our lifetime, and some were closer than what we could imagine, but we survived. It may have not been as we wanted it, but are we breathing?

I accept every day I am given, thank my creator, hug my loved ones, and put the biggest smile on my face. Am I unemployed? Yes. Was I on unemployment compensation? Yes. Did we lose a home to the economy? Yes. Am I paying a ton of money at the gas pumps? Yes. Am I disappointed in how things are going? No.

Friends look at your circumstances from a different standpoint. I am definitely NOT in the same position as I was four years ago, but I am in a "better place" than I was then.

Tough times make us realize what we have, and this does not concern material things. This is about life. Loved ones coming home from overseas, friends getting jobs, others fighting a deadly illnesses, donating time to a cause, helping someone from total depression, guiding others to the right course to take for aging, or hugging a grandchild and getting a hug back. NOW, that is what this is all about in life.

Look at your own life and see what you consider important. If you have to physically touch it, and it doesn't move, does it mean anything or is it that important to us? Sorry for the long statement, but this has been a concern for a long time.

## The Marriage

Dad told me the story of how he and Mom got married. It started when Dad was in the Army and transferred to Ft. Leavenworth, KS. He stopped home for a visit and asked Mom to run away with him to Kansas. After he left and a little time later, Mom jumped a train to Kansas. The childhood sweethearts eloped. They had some time together before Dad shipped overseas to India.

Alone, Mom went back home to Illinois and face the music from the family. Under the circumstances, there were questions to be answered, but overall, it turned out well, and Mom did all she could be prepare for her husband's return.

When Dad came home, his parents, being good Catholics, said they HAD to remarry in the "Church." Being as Mom was not Catholic; the Pastor told them they could not have a ceremony in the church, so they were married in the rectory. This satisfied Dad's family, and he was now back in their good graces.

They faced many hardships in their first years of marriage, but the love they shared grew to be rock solid for over 60 plus years. Believe me when I say it was not always fantastic, but they knew how to overcome their problems a few of which I have written about before. Every time I look at their wedding photo, it engulfs me in warmth and love. To me it represents everything they stood for and the drive to make it. God bless, love, and keep them both.

## Sandy

Sunday is a day dedicated to family, unless you have a storm looming upon the horizon. Pack things up, get rid of anything that will fly, stock up on water and non-perishables, fill the gas tank, charge your phones, cook up some meals in advance, cuddle together, hug tight, and watch some football. You never know what it will present. Prepare for the worse, and rejoice over the best. Have a great day in spite it all.

## The Storm

The weather here in New England is interesting if not fascinating. It provides us with tons of emotion, such as fear, relief, and disappointment. Fear is center focus for the storm coming and the potential damage it could do. The feeling of personal relief is there because the storm is not directing itself at Rhode Island. I personally have the feeling of disappointment for this storm is preventing my oldest son, whom I have not seen in a couple of years, from attending a conference in Boston so we could have lunch together and visit. In any case, the feeling of hope is overwhelming me for those who are in harm's way. I pray that they are safe and remain so throughout this experience. My personal feelings are immaterial compared to everyone else. My thoughts and prayers are with you all and will remain there until we are able rejoice together. Please stay in touch as long as you can. I will remain in touch as long as I can. God bless you all.

## Happy Halloween, 2012

Halloween is a night we show our courage to face strangers and tell them we want a treat or we are going to play a trick on them.

Think back when we were their age. Did we have the guts to put on a costume that makes us look completely different from what we normally look like and demand something from someone with whom we have little to no daily contact? The greatest part is that we get something for nothing.

I remember when I went out Trick or Treating; I was scared half to death even though Dad was behind me, my sister, and best friend were next to me. The only thing I was looking forward to was Mrs. O'Connor's fudge. That was gold to us kids. It has to have been award winning. It was so good. Her and her sisters made from scratch. Remembering coming home, emptying the bag on the living room floor, and sorting thought the loot. Mom and Dad would comment about the precious package of fudge. I don't know how it happened, but there was always an extra package, which they claimed as theirs. Mrs. O'Connor took care of them too.

They did their in depth scan of our loot, removed anything that was not wrapped, and gave their blessings to divide the stuff into daily allowances. This was "sugar" control.

Being a kid back then was fun but controlled, rationed, and monitored. We lived and enjoyed every single minute of it. So did Mom and Dad.

## Turkey Month

It is officially Turkey month. The ghosts and goblins have been stored for another year. The Horn of Plenty is now on display along with our normal pilgrims, Native Americans, turkeys, pumpkin pies, sweet potatoes, and cranberry sauce. Preparing for a major holiday season of the year always brings excitement.

The one thing we need to keep in mind with all of these activities is sharing with others less fortunate than we are. There are many who need our help, especially now. Please don't forget we all came into this world naked and without a thing to our name. We depended on others to get us through those times. There are many others who are in the same position, now. They may not be an infant, but they are still in need of help.

PLEASE look deep inside and help in any way you can whether it be a food, money, clothing, or time donation. If you cannot do anything at this time, try to budget a little each week to be able to help in some way or sometime. Not only will you be aiding others, but you will also be helping yourself to be a better person.

## NON-PAID NON-POLITICAL ANNOUNCEMENT

If I were asked to run for office and write a campaign speech, the background would include assessing the opponent and their record, determining their strong and weak points. If they were the incumbent, I would also study the positive and negative events in their term in office. THEN build a platform on what my term would do to help improve the way of life in my district and create realistic plans on how to get it done. These plans would include the difference compared to what is currently being done. All of this needs to be answered before I would even open my mouth to anyone about running. If there were nothing I could do better, I wouldn't run.

If I could make a difference, I would have a future in politics (GOD FORBID). My platform and plan would need to be in black and white, made a part of every printed piece that was distributed, and in every speech. This is something that would not change from day one to Election Day. Would I try to slam my opponent? Why should I if I believe in my plan? Would I talk about everything they did wrong or disliked by the people, hit their weak points, or degrade their time in office? NO. This does not communicate my plan. The opposition can do all the dirt digging and slamming they want. If they dig deep enough, they would probably come up with something.

With this said, I ONLY vote for people who talk about what their goal, their plan, their vision, and their guide is to get it done. If they were not in office, I already know what the incumbent did. I just want to know exactly what the new person is going to do to improve it, PERIOD!

This personal slamming, review of all the negatives, telling me that it will be more of the same, is only a way of INSULTING my intelligence, and I take THAT personally. I can read, listen, study, investigate, and even take action myself, so I do not need someone telling me what I already know. I need them to tell me HOW they are going execute their plan. I want to read it, hold it, and buy into it. I do not want to hear the words "they will fix it" without backup. If you presented to your boss a sales plan with just the words "it will get better" without anything to support it, do you think this would be acceptable? I think not. In addition, if this is the only thing they have to run on as a platform, they do not deserve my vote or any ones vote. Just saying.

## Sandy

The impact of tropical storm Sandy was overwhelming. Even though we were not personally affected, thank our dear Lord, there are friends who were wiped out. Sunday, as they prepared for this storm, put things in order, and even left their home for safety, the wrath of this hurricane was unforgiving. Having a wingspan of 800 miles, it has to be one of the largest weapons of mass destruction. It was not even one from a terrorist, unless Mother Nature changed her affiliation.

Billions of dollars in destruction, hundreds of miles of coastline gone, cities filled in sand, tunnels overflowing with water, transportation at a standstill, no electricity for thousands, trees now a part of the interior decorations or carrying racks on cars, families wondering how they are going to put things together, businesses determining if they will ever reopen (most of which are small businesses), or even something as simple as enough gas in the tank to sit in line for hours before it can be filled.

For all of you affected by Sandy, you are in our prayers and thoughts. For you who lived through it and are in good shape, thank your Creator and look for ways to help others. For you who were not affected at all from this storm, realize how fortunate you are and still look for ways to help those less fortunate. Love always triumphs over disaster.

## Sunday Football

Sundays always give me fantastic memories. When my kids were much younger, fall Sundays were pre-set for home activities. Sunday mass was necessary. Breakfast was out at a restaurant or cooked at home on either the grill or the stovetop. After cleanup, it was the ritual of lighting a fire in the fireplace, getting the hot dogs, buns, chips, salsa, munchies, and beverages laid out, and setting up a comfy spot to prepare for SUNDAY FOOTBALL.

My daughter and sons would claim their areas early, and Dad was always left with remain space. Being in the Midwest, the games started at noon, the second game at 3:30 pm, and 60 Minutes was "watched in its entirety at its regularly scheduled time." The participants depended on who wanted to show up. We roasted hot dogs and marshmallows in the fireplace and ate our way through a football-filled day. We planned, prepared, and executed with perfection our fall Sundays.

Thank God, my wife is a sports fan who lived her life in a similar way. We still spend our Sundays watching football from 1:00 pm until midnight. Gotta love that game! I will hold this one thing near and dear to my heart. We were together, had fun, screamed our lungs out, and laughed at each other. That is what counted.

## New Week

There is nothing like a great weekend to get you started for the beginning of another week. Spending time with family or friends; getting together for a sporting event; gathering with loved ones at a local pub, restaurant, church, or home; playing games with the kids, grandkids, nieces, nephews, brothers, or sisters; or just plainly reading a book or writing an personal article to publish on Facebook, it all leads to doing something that gives you pleasure.

Pleasure leads to relaxation and rejuvenation. R&R with exercise are supposed to release endorphins, and that is to give you good mental health. Good mental health makes for a great attitude to approaching the new week with a lesser tendency to cause bodily harm to the first person to approach you with a cheery smile.

**Election Day**

Need I say how important this day is to every one? There is no excuse for not voting. We received this privilege to determine the direction of our country, lives, and well-being. If you do not have a means of getting to your polling place or do not know where to vote, call your Board of Elections, City Hall, Councilman, or anyone who might be running for office. They will see that you get to where you need to be.

Vote for the person you feel will do the best job and NOT most popular. Your honesty provides the peace of mind that you did the right thing, no matter who wins. If your candidate did not win, you have every right to complain about how things are going. On the other hand, if your person is a winner, support what made you confident they were the right person for the job.

Remember, voting for the most popular person is NOT ALWAYS the best choice. A real bonus is voting for the person who you feel is most qualified and popular. My only request is to vote intelligently and diligently.

**The Aftermath**

THANK GOD, IT IS OVER! Our television commercials will now return to the mundane product related promotions and not hear a performance report on a candidate. We can now go to the mailbox and receive our bills and advertising without the hundreds of political leaflets. I have been shredding them as they arrive and have now filled another container. We can also drive down the street and see the houses and businesses without the signs covering everything up.

Are you going to miss that non-solicited knock at the door or phone call disrupting your meals? Can life now return to normal whatever that may be?

This election was unbelievable considering the money spent, the amount of travel and advertising done, the number of people involved in all campaigns, and the stress on every citizen in this country. Now it all falls on our leader to take us to that next step toward achieving that goal of the American Dream. Let us all pray that he guides toward the recovery of our great nation. It is also up to us to support him as best as we can.

## The Market

I was at the market today (shock). I think people believe I live at the market, but this is where I get my best material. People are people when they are buying food. Go figure. The problem is not the actions of people but their attitudes. The people who work the counters, packers, runners, stockers, information people, etc. are human beings and are deserving of respect.

I witnessed something that I never want to see again. A patron was giving the checkout person and bagger a mouthful because of a problem with the register, which caused her lose 3 MINUTES of her time. I was the only person in line behind her. I cannot imagine the scene that could have erupted if there was a larger audience. If she was running short of time, she should have just left. She blew for something of which no one had control. There is such a thing as forgiveness or patience. The total time it took to get it fixed was a matter of three minutes. The cashier apologized and looked embarrassed. The bagger had the look of fear. I had the look of anger and disgust.

Respect! How were we brought up? If we are introduced to someone for the first time, what do we say? If someone we cannot stand confronts us, how do we handle ourselves? If we have to do business with someone who is a complete a**h***, what do we do? These situations occur every day; it is how we deal with them that show our maturity. HOW MATURE ARE WE?

## Hurricane vs. Tornado

I will say I thought I would be more relaxed with a hurricane over a tornado. The fear factor for a tornado is short lived, but it is traumatizing. Once notified of the possibility of a watch alert that follows with a warning alert, that is all there is to it. If the unfortunate happens, it is over in seconds. The damage is done and the rebuilding can be estimated and planned. I know that sounds cold, but I have lived through those times, saw the effects, and, yes, attended funerals for friends who did not make it.

I will admit Sandy was a real revelation. The warning time is a positive thing, knowing and preparing for what is going to happen, the precautions taken, the supplies stored, and thoughts of any loose ends. I think the emotional strain comes from the amount of time of the original notice to the first drop of rain.

When it arrives, it takes a while for the energy to build, preparing for the devastation, and then watching the destruction a little at a time. Seeing trees down, boats smashed, piers and roads washed away, cars floating like buoys, homes and business consumed in water, sand, and mud, and wondering what else can happen. It can take a matter of a few hours or, like in Sandy and Katrina's case, almost a whole day. Little by little, a complete section of the country is gone.

I think both present their own form of disaster. One is pin pointed and immediate, and the other is massive and prolonged. Both will leave us with power outages, clean up measures, insurance battles, health concerns, and emotional rebuilding. The unnerving thing about a hurricane is the time it takes to arrive, the amount of time to pass through the area, and then the aftermath of its rage. It all takes its toll on the nerves. This is not taking under consideration the time spent indoors watching all of the devastation happen before your eyes knowing there is nothing you can do except pray.

## A Love Story, The Beginning

My wife and I found each other on Match.com. We both had experienced many personalities, strange beings, and living things all of which fall under the classification of the human race. It reached the point that the feeling of being alone for the rest of our lives sounded good. It became a crossroads with the membership. Do we continue or stop? Separately we both said one more time, if it happens great, if not, we quit.

One evening after work, sitting in the apartment with the lap top open checking my emails, there was a notice from Match.com about a potential match. Being intrigued, I opened up the profile and began reading. The words written were amazing. Almost as if she were sitting right here talking to me. I felt the warmth of her words in my heart. At the end, I wished it were not over. I wanted more.

I responded with the usually acknowledge and interest in her profile. She returned a response that night. We exchanged personal email addresses and this began our email-pal relationship. We got to the point of calling it "Topic De Jour. We covered topics of likes and dislikes, pasts, family, occupations, occupational hazards, parents, siblings, children, their trials and tribulations, previous relationships, pervious spouses and marriages, ups, downs, and anything that can be discussed without having to look into each others' eyes.

This continued for 4 months on a daily basis without phone contact. In a way, it was safe and enjoyable because we knew we had winners on each end of the connection. The "Loser" tag didn't exist which made it even more enjoyable. The realization hit both of us that we were not trying to impress each other with looks, money, toys, sex, or forced conversation leading to egos, lies, and fronts. We were just us, period.

Finally, we proposed a face-to-face meeting. Now another level of excitement entered the relationship. It was the feeling like this was going to be the make it or break it stage. We were either going to love what we see or hate what we see. We determined that is would be logical to meet somewhere just for coffee. This would make it not an investment like a dinner, but something that had no cost involved, so walking away would be easy and painless. We both laughed at our cynicism, but exchanged phone numbers.

The first time I heard her voice was like magic. The tone inflections were like music. We laughed at the fact that it took us four months to get to this stage when for others, it would be a farewell coffee. We agreed to meet at Barnes & Noble on Bald Hill Road on July 27th at 7:00PM. We exchanged our attire for that evening so we would recognize each other. The countdown started as the excitement built. All the while, we still emailed daily.

The evening of the 27th arrived. My heart was pounding as if I was going to perform at the Met for the first time in my life. This is going to be a first date with someone with whom I fell in love without setting eyes on her. I fell in love with her inner self. I couldn't wait to meet her entirety. Like a dream come true.

I arrived at Barnes & Noble around 6:50 PM to see if I can catch a glimpse of her when she comes through the doors. It felt like I was cheating, but I was happy to be finally meeting the one person who touched my heart. I felt like a kid on Christmas waiting for Santa to arrive. Palms were moist, tongue dry, heart beating hard and rapid, and a silly grin on my face. I must have looked like a maniac standing behind display of books right in the middle aisle staring at the front door. Every time someone came through, my heart skipped a beat.

Almost 7:00 PM on the nose, This vision of beauty walked in the store wearing the exactly what she said she would (I even remember what it was). She glanced around and proceeded to the coffee shop. My excitement was overflowing as I followed her. I felt like a stalker, but in a way, I could not wait to say, "Hi, I'm Tony." I stood behind her and waited for her to order her coffee when I said to make that two, then turned to her and said my opening line, along with, "You must be Carol."

My heart was racing. I know my face was 90 shades of red, and possibly a little sweat to make it glisten. I have stood in front of hundreds of people to speak, but to stand in front of someone who has become my best friend over the past four months, knows more about me than even my parents, and holds my heart in her hands, to just say seven little well rehearsed words was more exhilarating than anything. Her voice sent me into the clouds.

We got our coffees, went to a table along the wall, and started talking. We covered everything from our emails to everyday life and more. Our conversation was as if we were old friends and catching up from the last time we were together. That may have been true had it not been that afternoon since we last emailed each other.

At 11:00 PM the store manager informed us they were closing and requested us to leave. As we walked out in the parking lot, we continued to talk. It must have been fate, because our cars were parked one car width away from each other. We leaned against our cars continuing our conversation. When a city police car pulled up behind us and asked if everything was all right. I looked at my watch to see it was about 2:00 AM. We looked at each other and burst out laughing. We told the cop we were fine and nothing was wrong. He laughed and left us, only to realize everyone else had gone home, and the only two cars left in the lot were ours.

We both had to be at work in less than six hours. Our farewell consisted of us making plans for Thursday night when a special Water Fires was held in Providence's Waterplace Park. The most memorable part of the farewell was saying "Good night" and not good-bye. There was no kiss, hug or awkward sign of affection because the feeling inside was better than any clumsy act to say its over. It was just a "To Be Continued" farewell.

## A Love Story, Date Two

The day of our second date seemed like an eternity. The clock was not moving. The second hand took an hour to make one rotation. Everyone in the office kept asking me if everything was all right because I must have had a smile on my face that did not fade. Nothing seemed to bother me even when bad news of a potential quality problem that might delay the samples for a tradeshow. I calmly discussed an alternative if the problem becomes a reality. I had to admit, I was in love.

Once home, clothes changed, and making sure I had everything needed, i.e., wallet, money, car keys, jacket, cell phone, zipper zipped, address, directions, and phone number. I was all set. The only thing that could go wrong is to get lost, which is totally a possibility for this is the first venture to that part of the city.

It was a beautiful evening, sun out which meant a moon and stars will be visible. A light breeze was blowing. This might mean a chilly night. All the while not thinking of where I am going and missed a turn. Now I needed to back track to a familiar spot and start over. Time was not on my side. Decision time, should I be macho and see if I make the correct turn or call and ask the right way to go. It all depends on ego. I have never had this ego thing going for me, so I made a phone call.

Her son answered the phone. I introduced myself; he did the same; and directions were requested. He sounded a little apprehensive in his answer, but gave them any way. I understood about his being protective because of his mother's recent acquaintances. I proceeded to follow his instructions to a tee. I arrived at the ugly yellow house on the left, second from the corner.

As I got out of the car, the son met me in the yard and informed me his mother would be here shortly. We talked about the directions especially the description of the final leg of the trip. We laughed and got to know each other, which, I think, put his mind at ease about me not being a deviant pervert from the Midwest taking his mother out.

Prior to my arrival, he had a discussion with her about the Water Fires event that evening. He thought they were always held on a Friday or Saturday. She informed him that this was a special event held on this Thursday evening. It would be less crowed and allow us to continue talking. He confirmed this when we were talking and also through a little research later.

When she came out of the house, sweater and purse in hand, she looked radiant with a smile that took my breath away. After a few more minutes of talking with the son. I shook hands with the son and smiled at him trying to reassure that my intentions with his mother were strictly good and love related. He smiled and said, "Have a good time." That phrase made all tension disappear.

The downtown evening was slightly on the warm side with a warm breeze. We decided not to take our jacket and sweater along. If we get cold, we will just return to the car and pick them up. As we walked to the park, we talked with relaxed feelings as if we had known each other for years. We found each other's hand and held on tight.

Once we got to the part of the park where the fireplaces were set up, there is a restaurant and lounge who opened their patio for visitors to enjoy a drink or food during the presentation. We both had glass of wine, sipping and talking along the railing overlooking the fires. Once dark set in the beauty of the fire reflection off the water, the smell of burning wood, and the heat that is emitted seemed to warm the entire area.

We talked like we had not seen each other for ages. Our laughter was sincere and felt wonderful to be able to feel so relaxed being together. Soon the fires were burning down, so I put my arm around her to hold her close. At first it was for warmth, but as the evening went on, it was a need for us to be closer together.

We turned around to see who was left in the patio area to discover we were the only ones there. Looking at the huge clock on the outside wall, it read 1:30 AM. We did it again. We both needed to be at work in a little over six hours. We laughed and started back to the car. When we reached a point on the path around the water, I stopped, held her in my arms, our lips met, and the world stood still. We knew this was the beginning of a relationship for which we both had been searching.

Finally, our quest was over. That night we took off our "Losers Wanted" signs from our foreheads and replaced them with "Happily Taken" signs. This was the beginning of the love story of a lifetime. We are blessed to be the main characters.

# CONCLUSION

In the beginning, there is an end in sight. The only difference is, the true ending has not been determined yet. As long as my mind is functional, my fingers or voice can retell stories and these are still connected to my heart, it will continue to produce words of wisdom, memories, and radiate rays of love.

There are more entries waiting to be shared on paper or cyber screens. The true purpose of this is not money, wealth, or fame. It is to leave something of me for my children and grandchildren, help anyone who might need a little pick-me-up, a direction to be pointed for someone to find themselves, a lesson in loving ourselves and others, or just putting a smile on faces to pass along to some else who will do the same.

**NOT THE END, BUT TO BE CONTINUED . . .**

Thank you for all being a friend, which is something that should be highly cherished these days. I would love to hear comments and suggestions. I can be reached at:

Email:              tonyb@lifesjourneyresources.com

Facebook pages:   Tony Bovi

                    Life's Journey Resources, LLC

Twitter:           @tony3595

Tumbr:             Life's Journey.tumblr